INTRODUCTION TO THE
PSALMS

INTRODUCTION TO THE
PSALMS

A Song from Ancient Israel

NANCY L. DECLAISSÉ-WALFORD

CHALICE
PRESS

ST. LOUIS, MISSOURI

Biblical quotations, unless otherwise noted, are from the New Revised Standard Version Bible, copyright 1989, Division of Christian Education of the National Council of the Churches of Christ in the United States of America. Used by permission. All rights reserved.

Scripture marked NASB is taken from the NEW AMERICAN STANDARD BIBLE ®, © Copyright The Lockman Foundation 1960, 1962, 1963, 1968, 1971, 1972, 1973, 1975, 1977, 1995. Used by permission.

Image on page 1, "MS. Lat. liturg. e.47, fol. 30v," is from BODLEIAN LIBRARY, UNIVERSITY OF OXFORD. Used by permission of Bodleian Library, University of Oxford.

Maps on pages 47 and 49, "Plate 15 Babylonian Empire" and "Plate 16 Persian Empire," by Margaret Jordan Brown are from THE MERCER DICTIONARY OF THE BIBLE, copyright © 1990 by Mercer University Press. Used by permission of Mercer University Press.

Cover art: © Tate Gallery, London/Art Resource, NY/Art Resource
Cover and interior design: Elizabeth Wright

This book is printed on acid-free, recycled paper.

Visit Chalice Press on the World Wide Web at
www.chalicepress.com

10 9 8 7 6 5 4 3 2 1   04   05   06   07   08   09

Library of Congress Cataloging-in-Publication Data

DeClaissé-Walford, Nancy L., 1954-
  Introduction to the Psalms : a song from ancient Israel / Nancy L. deClaissé-Walford.
    p. cm.
  Includes bibliographical references and index.
  ISBN 0-827216-23-8 (pbk. : alk. paper)
  ISBN 978-0-827216-23-8
  1. Bible. O.T. Psalms—Introductions. I. Title.
  BS1430.52.D43 2004
  223'.2061—dc22

                                                    2004014434

CONTENTS

PREFACE

In the fall of 1991, I began doctoral studies at Baylor University in Waco, Texas. Over the next few years, my advisor, W. H. Bellinger Jr., introduced me to the study of the Hebrew Psalter. My dissertation, which subsequetly took the form of a book published by Mercer Univesity Press, was titled *Reading from the Beginning: The Shaping of the Hebrew Psalter.* My purpose in that undertaking was to discover clues to the shape and shaping of the Book of Psalms. I asked, "Why these 150 psalms, in this particular order in the Psalter? Why does Psalm 1 begin the Book? Why is Psalm 90 located where it is?" And so forth. The work was fascinating. And much remains to be learned and discovered.

This work, *Introduction to the Psalms: A Song from Ancient Israel,* seeks to provide the reader with a solid introduction to the Hebrew Psalter, one that is informed by an interest in its shape and shaping. After an Introductory chapter, I examine in successive chapters the poetic style of the psalms in the Psalter, their *Gattungen,* the broad shape of the book, and the history of its shaping. Beginning with chapter 5, I study each book of the Psalter, pausing at points to examine in detail individual psalms which are either key to the shaping of the Psalter, important examples of their *Gattung,* or interesting studies in poetic syle. The final chapter is titled, "How Then Shall We Read the Psalter?", and summarizes the conclusions of the previous chapters and proposes a way to read the Psalter as a unified whole. Two appendicies povide a listing of the Superscriptions and *Gattungen* of the psalms in the Hebrew Psalter and an explanation of many of the techical terms found in their superscriptions

Thanks and gratitude are due many. The McAfee School of Theology at Mercer University, under the leadership of Dean R. Alan Culpepper, generously granted me a sabbatical leave during the spring and summer sessions of 2003. My colleagues a the school filled in the gaps in my teaching schedule and administrative duties during this time. My editor at Chalice Press, Jon Berquist, was enthusiastic and supportive about the project. The Society of Biblical Literature Book of Psalms Section has graciously listened to my presentations and input at meetings of the section for the past ten years. And of course, no project would be possible without the love and support of my family: my husband Steve and my sons Calvin and Aaron. Yes, Mom's in her study again. Yes. Mom's writing another book. They are my firm grounding in the real world, and there is no substitute for that kind of influence on the writing endeavor.

But perhaps my deepest gratitude should be to those ancient Israelite poets who first sang the songs that I find myself so carefully studying. And to the ancient communtites of faith who took those songs and shaped them into the book that has been handed down to us. The Hebrew Psalter tells a story of faith and struggle, of despair and hope, a song that sings to all of us across the millennia.

Nancy L. deClaissé-Walford
Atlanta, Georgia

An illuminated manuscript of one of the psalms.
Courtesy of the Bodleian Library, University of Oxford

Introduction

The book of Psalms is perhaps the most well-known and best-loved of the books of the Hebrew Bible. Words like "The LORD is my shepherd" (23:1); "O LORD, you have searched me and known me" (139:1); "My God, my God, why have you forsaken me?" (22:1); and "Bless the LORD, O my soul" (104:1) ring familiar in our ears.

In the Jewish faith, the Psalms are valued as the songs of King David, the tenth-century B.C.E. king of ancient Israel, and they are read at every synagogue service. The rabbis wrote, "Whatever David says in his book pertains to himself, to all Israel, and to all times."[1] The New Testament contains some sixty-nine quotations from the book of Psalms, including:

The stone that the builders rejected
has become the cornerstone;
this was the Lord's doing,
    and it is amazing in our eyes.
(Mk. 12:10–11=Ps. 118:22–23)

I saw the Lord always before me,
    for he is at my right hand so that I will not be shaken;
therefore my heart was glad, and my tongue rejoiced;
    moreover my flesh will live in hope.
(Acts 2:25–26=Ps. 16:8–9)

Your throne, O God, is forever and ever,
    and the righteous scepter is the scepter of your kingdom.
You have loved righteousness and hated wickedness;
therefore God, your God, has anointed you
    with the oil of gladness beyond your companions.
(Heb. 1:8–9=Ps. 45:6–7)

Benedictine monks, following the Rule of Saint Benedict, recite the complete Psalter once each week and the psalms form the prayer life of the community.[2] The printed New Testament often includes the books of Proverbs and Psalms as something of a "preface" to the work. The *Revised Common Lectionary*, a guide for scripture reading in worship, lists a psalm for reading at nearly every worship occasion[3]; and the words of the Psalter are read at weddings, baptisms, funerals, and anniversaries.

"The Psalter"
"The book of Psalms"
Both are names for the collection of 150 poems found in the Jewish and Christian Bibles. The word "psalm" is from the Greek word ψαλμος, which means "hymn." "Psalter" means "a printed collection of hymns." The Hebrew title of the book is סֵפֶר תְּהִלִּים *(sēper tᵉhillîm)*, which means "book of hymns."

Perhaps the book of Psalms is so well-loved and well-used because of its unique nature. The Bible is described as "the word of God"—the words of the creator, redeemer, and sustainer of the world—to humanity. We read in its pages the story of creation, the stories of the ancestors and ancient Israel, the words of the prophets and the wisdom writers, the stories told by the gospel writers, and the words of the writers of the New Testament letters—words from God, via human agents, to God's created humanity. But we encounter something different in the Psalter. It pages record, for the most part, not the words of God to humanity, but the words of humanity to God. In it, we encounter striking second-person language, language found only rarely in the rest of the Bible. The words are meant to be spoken by people in the presence of and directly to God:

> Protect me, O God, for in you I take refuge. (16:1)

> Praise is due to you, O God, in Zion. (65:1)

> Let the heavens praise your wonders, O LORD, your faithfulness in the assembly of the holy ones. (89:5)

Nahum Sarna wrote these words in 1993:

> In the Psalms, the human soul extends itself beyond its confining, sheltering, impermanent house of clay. It strives for contact with the Ultimate Source of all life. It gropes for an experience of the divine Presence. The biblical psalms are essentially a record of the human quest for God.[4]

And Dietrich Bonhoeffer wrote during the first half of the twentieth century:

> Whoever has begun to pray the Psalter earnestly and regularly, will soon give leave to those other, easy, little prayers of their own because they lack the power, passion, and fire, to be found in the Psalter.[5]

Many scholars describe the book of Psalms as "the prayerbook of the second temple"; William L. Holladay titled his 1993 book about the Psalter *The Psalms through Three Thousand Years: Prayerbook of a Cloud of Witnesses*. The psalms are the prayers and songs of generations of Israelites who strove to define their relationship to and communicate with the God they called the Lord. The psalms encapsulate the joys, the grief, the questions, and the praises of our ancestors in the faith.

The psalms in the Hebrew Psalter come from many times and many places in the life of ancient Israel. We read the recorded history of the ancient Israelites in the pages of the Old Testament—Abraham and Sarah, Isaac and Rebekah, Rachel and Leah and Jacob, and Joseph; Moses and Miriam and Aaron and the exodus from Egypt; Saul and David and the kings of ancient Israel; the prophets—Isaiah, Hosea, Joel; the wisdom teachers—Solomon and Qoheleth; and the prophets of the exile and the return from exile. Psalms were composed, sung, preserved, and handed down during each of these periods in the history of ancient Israel.

Time Line of Ancient Israel

PREEXILLIC PERIOD						POSTEXILLIC PERIOD	
1800 Abraham and Sarah	1200 Exodus from Egypt	1000 David and Solomon	950 Divided Kingdom	722 Fall of Northern Kingdom	586 Fall of Southern Kingdom	538 Return from Exile	515 Temple rebuilt

Assigning a precise date to most of the psalms in the Psalter is extremely difficult, since a part of their beauty is their timelessness.[6] We can find clues within a few psalms, however, that indicate the general time frames of their original compositions. Psalm 45, for instance, was most likely composed in the pre-exilic period (before 587 B.C.E.) as a royal wedding song.[7]

> The princess is decked in her chamber with gold-woven robes;
>   in many-colored robes she is led to the king;
>   behind her the virgins, her companions, follow.
> With joy and gladness they are led along
>   as they enter the palace of the king. (45:13–15)

Psalm 81 probably originated in the northern kingdom of Israel between 950 and 722 B.C.E.[8]

> Hear, O my people, while I admonish you;
>   O Israel, if you would but listen to me!
> There shall be no strange god among you;
>   you shall not bow down to a foreign god. (81:8–9)

Psalms 74 and 79 most likely come from the exilic period of ancient Israel's history (between 587 and 538 B.C.E.).[9]

> O God, why do you cast us off forever?

> Why does your anger smoke against the sheep of your
> pasture?
> Remember your congregation, which you acquired long ago,
> which you redeemed to be the tribe of your heritage.
> (74:1–2)

And Psalm 119 can be dated to the postexilic period (after 538
B.C.E.).[10]

> Happy are those whose way is blameless,
> who walk in the law of the LORD.
> Happy are those who keep his decrees,
> who seek him with their whole heart,
> who also do no wrong,
> but walk in his ways. (119:1–3)

In the Second Temple period (after 515 B.C.E.), these prayers and
songs of ancient Israel were collected and ordered into the book we call
Psalms and placed within the canon of scripture.

Second Temple

The first Israelite temple was built in Jerusalem during the reign of
King Solomon (10th century B.C.E.). That temple was destroyed by
the Babylonians in 587 B.C.E. The temple was rebuilt around 515
B.C.E. by the Israelites who returned from captivity in Babylon. It is
this temple to which we refer as the Second Temple.

In that process, the Psalms underwent a transformation from being
the words of humankind to God into being scriptural words of God to
humankind. They became words of encouragement and hope to a
community in turmoil, a community coming to grips with a new life
situation.[11]

What are those words of encouragement and hope? What is the
story and message of the Psalter? We will begin by examining the
literary styles, forms, structures, and historical backgrounds of the psalms
in the Psalter. We will then explore each of the Psalter's five books,
pausing along the way to study individual psalms and groups of psalms.
Finally, we will attempt to draw some conclusions about the shape of
the Psalter and about its story and message.

Let us now turn to this book of hope and encouragement and seek to understand its words—words spoken and written to our ancestors in the faith and words written to communities of faith today.

1

What Words Are We Reading?

The Psalter is written in poetry rather than prose. How do we recognize poetry and how do we read it? Compare the following two passages:

> The library of Brown Middle School wants to encourage each student to check out and read at least twelve books during the upcoming school year. Imagine traveling to different times and places and meeting new and interesting people without spending a penny—what a great way to broaden your horizons, make you aware of the many possibilities your life holds, and help you understand other peoples' lives! Please participate in this program during the year, and we think you will agree that reading is a wonderful way to explore your world.

> There is no frigate like a book
> To take us lands away,
> Nor any coursers like a page
> Of prancing poetry.
> This traverse may the poorest take
> Without oppress of toll;
> How frugal is the chariot
> That bears the human soul![1]

The Nature of Poetry

The reader approaches prose and poetry in very different ways. The first passage above is prose. It is an invitation to students at Brown Middle School to come to the library and take advantage of a wonderful way to explore their world. The message of the second passage is the same—"Come, explore your world through books." But the second passage is poetry. How can we tell? How do we know when we are reading poetry? One author offers the following:

As soon as we perceive that a verbal sequence has a sustained rhythm, that it is formally structured according to a continuously operating principle of organization, we know that we are in the presence of poetry and we respond to it accordingly. We respond to it…expecting certain effects from it and not others, granting certain conventions to it and not others. All our experiences with language and literature, from the time we are small children, condition that discrimination.[2]

We learn then to identify poetry in several ways:

1. It looks different from prose on the page. Its lines are shorter; they don't fill the width of the page. Some lines are indented.
2. It has a certain rhythm or beat. We can describe the poem quoted above as having a 4/3 beat or rhythm:

> There **is** no **fri**-gate **like** a **book**
> To **take** us **lands** a-**way,**
> Nor **a**-ny **cour**-sers **like** a **page**
> Of **pranc**-ing **po**-e-**try**.

3. It uses metaphorical and imaginative language. A book is compared to a "frigate" in line one and a "chariot" in line seven; poetry is described as "prancing"; and the "human soul" is used as a synonym for "reader" in the last line of the poem.

Poetry in the Book of Psalms

When we open the pages of the Hebrew Bible, we see that the book of Psalms is laid out on the page differently from, say, the books of Genesis and Kings. Let's have a look at Psalm 3.

> O LORD, how many are my foes!
>   Many are rising against me…
> But you, O LORD, are a shield around me,
>   my glory, and the one who lifts up my head. (3:1, 3)

In Hebrew, the lines have a recognizable rhythm, what we may call a 3/3 pattern:

> *y^ehwāh māh rab-bû ṣā-râ*
> *rab-bîm qā-mîm ʿā-lâ…*
> *w^e-at-tāh y^ehwāh mā-gēn ba ʿa-dî*
> *k^e-bô-dî û-mē-rîm rō-ʾšî*
> (3:2, 4; MT 3:1, 3)

And Psalm 3 uses figurative language. The Lord is a "shield" to the psalmist (v. 3); the psalmist is not afraid of "ten thousand people" (v. 6); and the psalmist calls on God to "strike all my enemies on the cheek; break the teeth of the wicked" (v. 7).

Why are the psalms written in poetry? Walter Brueggemann titles a chapter in a book on poetry, "Poetry in a Prose-Flattened World."[3] What a statement—"A Prose-Flattened World"! Brueggemann is right. Our world is full of prose. We are bombarded daily with words—words that inform, instruct, guide, dictate, and attempt to persuade us. We become numb to the bombardment, and we tune out; we ignore. But when we encounter poetry, something happens to us; we tune in; we listen; we remember—the words to a song:

> We are travelers on a journey,
> fellow pilgrims on the road.
> We are here to help each other
> walk the mile and bear the load.
> I will hold the Christ-light for you
> in the nighttime of your fear.
> I will hold my hand out to you,
> speak the peace you long to hear.[4]

the rhythm of a poem:

> I shall be telling this with a sigh
> Somewhere ages and ages hence:
> Two roads diverged in a wood, and I—
> I took the one less traveled by,
> And that has made all the difference.[5]

and the imagery of a psalm:

> The LORD is my shepherd, I shall not want.
> He makes me lie down in green pastures;
> he leads me beside still waters;
> he restores my soul. (23:1–2)

Poetry draws us in, engages us, invites us to hear and remember. It is succinct, graphic, concrete. Walt Whitman wrote these words in the nineteenth century:

> After the seas are all cross'd,
> (as they seem already cross'd,)
> After the great captains and engineers have

accomplish'd their work,
After the noble inventors, after the scientists,
 the chemist, the geologist, the ethnologist,
Finally shall come the poet worthy that name,
The true son of God shall come singing his songs.[6]

Walter Brueggemann summarizes the matter well when he states that the power of poetry lies in its "shattering, evocative speech that breaks fixed conclusions and presses us always toward new, dangerous, imaginative possibilities."[7]

Hebrew Parallelism

The Psalter of the Hebrew Bible is composed in a special type (or genre) of poetry that was common throughout the ancient Near East. In addition to containing all of the elements of poetry that are discussed above, Hebrew poetry is made up of two or three parallel line units that are connected to one another in a number of ways. In the year 1779, Bishop Robert Lowth brought the phenomenon to the attention of the scholarly world:

> The correspondence of one Verse, or Line, with another I call Parallelism. When a proposition is delivered, and a second is subjoined to it, or drawn under it, equivalent, or contrasted with it, in sense; or similar to it in the form of Grammatical Construction; these I call Parallel Lines; and the words or phrases answering one to another in the corresponding Line Parallel Terms.[8]

Students of Hebrew poetry have been grappling with the concept of "parallelism" ever since. We will use a simple method of categorizing the ways in which the parallel line units are connected with one another. Observe the following examples:

Type One: Synonymous Parallelism
a) The earth is the LORD's and all that is in it,
 the world, and those who live in it. (Ps. 24:1)

b) You have turned my mourning into dancing;
 you have taken off my sackcloth and clothed me with joy. (30:11)

c) The Lord is my rock, my fortress, and my deliverer,
 my God, my rock in whom I take refuge,
 my shield, and the horn of my salvation, my stronghold. (18:2)

Type Two: Antithetic Parallelism
a) O let the evil of the wicked come to an end,
    but establish the righteous (7:9)

b) For you deliver a humble people,
    but the haughty eyes you bring down. (18:27)

c) Some take pride in chariots, and some in horses,
    but our pride is in the name of the LORD our God. (20:7)

Type Three: Synthetic Parallelism
a) Come and see what God has done:
    he is awesome in his deeds among mortals. (66:5)

b) From the rising of the sun to its setting
    the name of the LORD is to be praised. (113:3)

c) The wicked draw the sword and bend their bows
    to bring down the poor and needy,
    to kill those who walk uprightly. (37:14)

In Type One, "synonymous parallelism," the first line makes a statement, such as, "The earth is the LORD's and all that's in it," and the second (and sometimes a third) line reiterates—restates—the first, "the world and those who live in it."

In Type Two, "antithetic parallelism," the first line, as with Type One, makes a statement, like, "For you deliver a humble people." In Type Two, however, the next line (or lines) of the parallelism expresses an opposite thought: "but the haughty eyes you bring down."

In Type Three, "synthetic parallelism," the first line expresses a thought: "Come and see what God has done." The following line (or lines) further explains the meaning of the first line: "he is awesome in his deeds among mortals."

COMBINED OR MIXED TYPES

The types can be combined within their parallel lines. In Psalm 68:6, we read the following:

God gives the desolate a home to live in;
    he leads out the prisoners to prosperity,
    but the rebellious live in a parched land.

In this construction, lines one and two are synonymous, while line three is antithetic to both lines one and two. Look at Psalm 37:7:

> Be still before the LORD, and wait patiently for him;
>> do not fret over those who prosper in their way,
>> over those who carry out evil devices.

Here lines two and three are synonymous, and line one is set in synthetic parallelism with them.[9]

In all of the types—synonymous, antithetic, synthetic, and mixed—the two (or three) lines are to be read as a unit. A complete understanding of what the psalmist is saying comes from appropriating a single meaning from all of the lines read together.

Word Pairs

Another characteristic of Hebrew poetry is the occurrence of common word pairs within the parallel line units—what Bishop Lowth called "words or phrases answering one another in corresponding lines." Observe the words used in the line units of the opening verses of Psalm 49:

> Hear this, all you peoples;
>> give ear, all inhabitants of the world,
> both low and high,
>> rich and poor together.
> My mouth shall speak wisdom;
>> the meditation of my heart shall be understanding. (49:1–3)

In the first parallel structure, "hear" and "give ear" are paired, as are "peoples" and "inhabitants of the world." In the second parallel, "low and high" are paired with "rich and poor," and in the third, "my mouth" and "my heart" are paired, as are "wisdom" and "understanding." Psalm 92 provides additional examples:

> It is good to give thanks to the LORD
>> to sing praises to your name, O Most High;
> to declare your steadfast love in the morning
>> and your faithfulness by night,
> to the music of the lute and the harp,
>> to the melody of the lyre. (92:1–3)

In these three verses, we find a number of paired words: "give thanks" and "sing praises," the LORD" and "O Most High," "steadfast love" and "faithfulness," "morning" and "night," "music" and "melody," and "lute and harp" and "lyre." Finally, observe these verses from Psalm 21:

In your strength the king rejoices, O LORD,
    and in your help how greatly he exults!
You have given him his heart's desire
    and have not withheld the request of his lips...
Your hand will find out all your enemies;
    your right hand will find out those who hate you...
You will destroy their offspring from the earth,
    and their children from among humankind. (21:1–2, 8, 10)

Here, "strength" is paired with "help," "rejoices" with "exults," "given" with "not withheld," "desire" with "request," "hand" with "right hand," "enemies" with "those who hate you," "offspring" with "children," and "the earth" with "among humankind."

During the past two hundred years, students of Hebrew poetry have devoted a great deal of time to the study of word pairs. Some suggest that there existed in the ancient Near East a kind of thesaurus of acceptable word pairs that poets consulted as they composed their works. Far more likely is that the phenomenon of word pairs came about as the result of the unique character of the poetry—its structure of parallel line units. The frequently-used word pairs are a natural result of that structure.

Chiasmus

Hebrew poets also used certain structural elements in the composition of the psalms. One such structural element is called chiasmus—a reversal in the order of words in two otherwise parallel phrases. Observe the following chiastic lines:

For the LORD <u>knows</u> *the way of the righteous,*
    But *the way of the wicked* <u>will perish</u>. (1:6, NASB)

Here the psalmist has reversed the order of the words in line two so that the verbs occur at the beginning and the end of the two lines, while "the way of the righteous" and "the way of the wicked" are at the center of the construction.

In my distress <u>I called</u> *upon the LORD;*
    to my God <u>I cried for help</u>. (18:6)

In the above example, the two prepositional phrases "upon the LORD" and "to my God" are placed at the center of the parallel lines.

Every day I will bless you,
and praise your name *forever and ever.* (145:2)

Each line of this verse consists of two phrases. The reversal of the phrases in the second line creates a perfect chiastic structure.

Inclusio

A related structural element in Hebrew poetry is the inclusio—beginning and ending a particular unit of poetry in the same or similar ways. We may describe verse 2 of Psalm 145, which we examined just above, as having an inclusio structure as well as a chiastic structure. The first line begins with an adverbial phrase, "every day," and the second line ends with one, "forever and ever." Inclusios are also used on a larger scale. The magnificent creation poem in Psalm 8 begins and ends with the words:

O LORD, our Sovereign,
how majestic is your name in all the earth! (8:1, 9)

And in Book One of the Psalter, which includes Psalms 1–41, Psalm 1 and Psalm 41, the two psalms at the edges of the Book, begin with the word "happy"—אַשְׁרֵי (*'ašrê*):

Happy—אַשְׁרֵי (*'ašrê*)—are those who do not follow the advice of the wicked. (1:1)

Happy—אַשְׁרֵי (*'ašrê*)—are those who consider the poor. (41:1)

Acrostic Poetry

Another fascinating structural element of Hebrew poetry is the acrostic, where the lines or group of lines of a psalm begin with a successive letter of the Hebrew alphabet.[10] Psalms 25, 34, 111, 112, 119, and 145 are acrostic psalms, as is the wonderful poem in Proverbs 31:10–31. Observe the structure of Psalm 111:

111:1   הַלְלוּ יָהּ |

(א)   אוֹדֶה יְהוָה בְּכָל־לֵבָב

(ב)   בְּסוֹד יְשָׁרִים וְעֵדָה:

(ג)   2 גְּדֹלִים מַעֲשֵׂי יְהוָה

(ד)   דְּרוּשִׁים לְכָל־חֶפְצֵיהֶם׃

(ה)   3 הוֹד־וְהָדָר פָּעֳלוֹ

(ו)   וְצִדְקָתוֹ עֹמֶדֶת לָעַד׃

(ז)   4 זֵכֶר עָשָׂה לְנִפְלְאֹתָיו

(ח)   חַנּוּן וְרַחוּם יְהוָה׃

(ט)   5 טֶרֶף נָתַן לִירֵאָיו

(י)   יִזְכֹּר לְעוֹלָם בְּרִיתוֹ׃

(כ)   6 כֹּחַ מַעֲשָׂיו הִגִּיד לְעַמּוֹ

(ל)   לָתֵת לָהֶם נַחֲלַת גּוֹיִם׃

(מ)   7 מַעֲשֵׂי יָדָיו אֱמֶת וּמִשְׁפָּט

(נ)   נֶאֱמָנִים כָּל־פִּקּוּדָיו׃

(ס)   8 סְמוּכִים לָעַד לְעוֹלָם

(ע)   עֲשׂוּיִם בֶּאֱמֶת וְיָשָׁר׃

(פ)   9 פְּדוּת ׀ שָׁלַח לְעַמּוֹ

(צ)   צִוָּה־לְעוֹלָם בְּרִיתוֹ

(ק)   קָדוֹשׁ וְנוֹרָא שְׁמוֹ׃

(ר) 10 רֵאשִׁית חָכְמָה ׀ יִרְאַת יְהוָה

(שׁ)   שֵׂכֶל טוֹב לְכָל־עֹשֵׂיהֶם

(ת)   תְּהִלָּתוֹ עֹמֶדֶת לָעַד׃

The characters in parentheses along the right margin are the letters of
the Hebrew alphabet. Each line of Psalm 111 begins with its
corresponding letter of the alphabet in "abc" order.

Psalm 119 is an acrostic poem on a grand scale. It is divided into
8–verse stanzas. The eight lines in each stanza all begin with the same
letter of the Hebrew alphabet. Verses 81–88 begin with the Hebrew
letter כ, equivalent to English "k"; verses 89–96 begin with the Hebrew
letter ל, equivalent to English "l"; and verses 97–104 begin with מ,
equivalent to "m."

(כ)   81   כָּלְתָה לִתְשׁוּעָתְךָ נַפְשִׁי לִדְבָרְךָ יִחָלְתִּי:

82   כָּלוּ עֵינַי לְאִמְרָתֶךָ לֵאמֹר מָתַי תְּנַחֲמֵנִי:

83   כִּי־הָיִיתִי כְּנֹאד בְּקִיטוֹר חֻקֶּיךָ לֹא שָׁכָחְתִּי:

84   כַּמָּה יְמֵי־עַבְדֶּךָ מָתַי תַּעֲשֶׂה בְרֹדְפַי מִשְׁפָּט:

85   כָּרוּ־לִי זֵדִים שִׁיחוֹת אֲשֶׁר לֹא כְתוֹרָתֶךָ:

86   כָּל־מִצְוֹתֶיךָ אֱמוּנָה שֶׁקֶר רְדָפוּנִי עָזְרֵנִי:

87   כִּמְעַט כִּלּוּנִי בָאָרֶץ וַאֲנִי לֹא־עָזַבְתִּי פִקּוּדֶיךָ:

88   כְּחַסְדְּךָ חַיֵּנִי וְאֶשְׁמְרָה עֵדוּת פִּיךָ:

(ל)   89   לְעוֹלָם יְהוָה דְּבָרְךָ נִצָּב בַּשָּׁמָיִם:

90   לְדֹר וָדֹר אֱמוּנָתֶךָ כּוֹנַנְתָּ אֶרֶץ וַתַּעֲמֹד:

91   לְמִשְׁפָּטֶיךָ עָמְדוּ הַיּוֹם כִּי הַכֹּל עֲבָדֶיךָ:

92   לוּלֵי תוֹרָתְךָ שַׁעֲשֻׁעָי אָז אָבַדְתִּי בְעָנְיִי:

93   לְעוֹלָם לֹא־אֶשְׁכַּח פִּקּוּדֶיךָ כִּי בָם חִיִּיתָנִי:

94   לְךָ־אֲנִי הוֹשִׁיעֵנִי כִּי פִקּוּדֶיךָ דָרָשְׁתִּי:

95   לִי קִוּוּ רְשָׁעִים לְאַבְּדֵנִי עֵדֹתֶיךָ אֶתְבּוֹנָן:

96 לְכָל תִּכְלָה רָאִיתִי קֵץ רְחָבָה מִצְוָתְךָ מְאֹד:

(מ) 97 מָה־אָהַבְתִּי תוֹרָתֶךָ כָּל־הַיּוֹם הִיא שִׂיחָתִי:

98 מֵאֹיְבַי תְּחַכְּמֵנִי מִצְוֹתֶךָ כִּי לְעוֹלָם הִיא־לִי:

99 מִכָּל־מְלַמְּדַי הִשְׂכַּלְתִּי כִּי עֵדְוֹתֶיךָ שִׂיחָה לִי:

100 מִזְּקֵנִים אֶתְבּוֹנָן כִּי פִקּוּדֶיךָ נָצָרְתִּי:

101 מִכָּל־אֹרַח רָע כָּלִאתִי רַגְלָי לְמַעַן אֶשְׁמֹר דְּבָרֶךָ:

102 מִמִּשְׁפָּטֶיךָ לֹא־סָרְתִּי כִּי־אַתָּה הוֹרֵתָנִי:

103 מַה־נִּמְלְצוּ לְחִכִּי אִמְרָתֶךָ מִדְּבַשׁ לְפִי:

104 מִפִּקּוּדֶיךָ אֶתְבּוֹנָן עַל־כֵּן שָׂנֵאתִי ׀ כָּל־אֹרַח שָׁקֶר:

Acrostics were challenging, and, I think, fun compositions for the gifted poets of the Hebrew scriptures. Acrostic compositions most likely began as a "memory device," a method of prompting the speaker in the oral recitation of the psalm. As we see in Psalm 119, the structure became quite sophisticated and stylized as time went by.

The acrostic form was also used to indicate that the psalm writer has said all there is to say on a given subject, having summed it up "from א to ת," "from A to Z." The acrostic Psalm 145 is a good example. It begins with the words, in its א line:

(א) I will extol you, my God and King,
and bless your name forever and ever. (145:1)

The psalm then goes on, in its acrostic lines, to call upon Israel and all creation to extol God and to bless God's name, to summarize—from א to ת—all that readers and hearers need to know about remembering who God is and praising God for who God is.

And so we begin with poetry—elevated, rhythmic, evocative language spoken by humans to their creator God. In the carefully and artistically crafted parallel lines of that poetry, we read words of praise, of despair, of hope, of vengeance, and of wonder. How were the words shaped? Where did they come from? That is the subject of the next chapter.

2

The Forms of the Psalms

The singers of the psalms express a wide range of emotions and feelings and address a wide variety of topics.

Praise the LORD!
>O give thanks to the LORD, for he is good;
>for his steadfast love endures forever. (106:1)

How long, O LORD? Will you hide yourself forever?
>How long will your wrath burn like fire? (89:46)

Deliver me from my enemies, O my God;
>protect me from those who rise up against me. (59:1)

Be merciful to me, O God, be merciful to me,
>for in you my soul takes refuge;
in the shadow of your wings I will take refuge,
>until the destroying storms pass by. (57:1)

Happy are those whose way is blameless,
>who walk in the law of the LORD.
Happy are those who keep his decrees,
>who seek him with their whole heart. (119:1)

The LORD is king! Let the earth rejoice;
>let the many coastlands be glad!
Clouds and thick darkness are all around him;
>righteousness and justice are the foundation of his throne.
>(97:1–2)

O LORD, do not rebuke me in your anger,
>or discipline me in your wrath.
Be gracious to me, O LORD, for I am languishing;

O LORD, heal me, for my bones are shaking with terror.
(6:1–2)

The heavens are telling the glory of God;
    and the firmament proclaims his handiwork.
Day to day pours forth speech,
    and night to night declares knowledge. (19:1–2)

Literary Types

In the early twentieth century, Hermann Gunkel, a Form Critical scholar, studied the psalms and classified them by literary type or genre (*Gattung*, in German).[1] Based on the work of Gunkel, we may identify four major *Gattungen* of psalms in the Psalter.

Form Criticism

Form Criticism attempts to identify and then classify the various types (*Gattungen*) of literature found in the biblical text in order to help place the texts within the lives of the people who preserved and handed them on and in order to aid in interpreting the texts.

Hymns

1. **Hymns of the Community** are songs that were sung during worship on holy days.[2] The hymns include a number of themes, including: praising God—הַלְלוּ יָהּ (*hal'lû yāh*)—for all that God does on behalf of the people and praising God for God's presence among the people. In Gunkel's words, "The predominant mood in all the Hymns is the enthusiastic but reverent adoration of the glorious and awe-inspiring God."[3] We find hymnic words in Psalm 105:

O give thanks to the LORD, call on his name,
    make known his deeds among the peoples.
Sing to him, sing praises to him;
    tell of all his wonderful works…
He is the LORD our God;
    his judgments are in all the earth.
He is mindful of his covenant forever,
    of the word that he commanded, for a thousand generations,
the covenant that he made with Abraham
    his sworn promise to Isaac,

which he confirmed to Jacob as a statute,
     to Israel as an everlasting covenant,
saying, "To you I will give the land of Canaan
     as your portion for an inheritance." (105:1–2, 7–11)

The words of Psalm 33 call on the people to bless the Lord with music and song:

Rejoice in the LORD, O you righteous.
     Praise befits the upright.
Praise the LORD with the lyre;
     make melody to him with the harp of ten strings.
Sing to him a new song;
     play skillfully on the strings, with loud shouts. (33:1–3)[4]

2. **Thanksgiving Hymns of the Individual** were addressed to God in the worship of ancient Israel, just as were Hymns of the Community.[5] But in these thanksgiving hymns, a single voice is present, praising God for goodness to or on behalf of that individual, usually for a deliverance from some trying situation. Gunkel describes the occasion on which these songs would have been offered: "A person is saved out of great distress, and now with grateful heart he brings a thank offering to Yahweh; it was customary that at a certain point in the sacred ceremony he would offer a song in which he expresses his thanks."[6]

I will extol you, O LORD, for you have drawn me up,
     and did not let my foes rejoice over me.
O LORD my God, I cried to you for help,
     and you have healed me.
O LORD, you brought up my soul from Sheol,
     restored me to life from among those gone down to the Pit.
     (30:1–3)

Praise the LORD!
I will give thanks to the LORD with my whole heart,
     in the company of the upright, in the congregation.
Great are the works of the LORD,
     studied by all who delight in them.
Full of honor and majesty is his work,
     and his righteousness endures forever. (111:1–3)

The Community Hymns and Individual Hymns of Thanksgiving contain a number of elements that help us to identify their form

(*Gattung*). While not all of the elements are found in all of the hymns, they provide a guide for reading these psalms:

a. an *Introduction,* in which the psalmist declares the intention of giving thanks and praising God
b. a *Narrative,* in which the psalmist tells what has happened to the psalmist that has prompted the words of praise
c. a *Conclusion,* in which the psalmist praises God for all that God has done on the psalmist's behalf [7]

In Psalm 33, a hymn of the community, the elements of the hymn are included as follows:

a. Introduction—verses 1–3

> Rejoice in the LORD, O you righteous.
>> Praise befits the upright.
> Praise the LORD with the lyre;
>> make melody to him with the harp of ten strings,
> Sing to him a new song;
>> play skillfully on the strings, with loud shouts.

b. Narrative—verses 4–19

> For the word of the LORD is upright,
>> and all his work is done in faithfulness.
> He loves righteousness and justice;
>> the earth is full of the steadfast love of the LORD.
> By the word of the LORD the heavens were made,
>> and all of their host by the breath of his mouth.
> He gathered the waters of the sea as in a bottle;
>> he put the deeps in storehouses...
> A king is not saved by his great army;
>> a warrior is not delivered by his great strength.
> The war horse is a vain hope for victory,
>> and by its great might it cannot save...
> (vv. 4–7, 16–17)

c. Conclusion—verses 20–22

> Our soul waits for the LORD;
>> he is our help and shield.
> Our heart is glad in him,
>> because we trust in his holy name.

Let your steadfast love, O LORD, be upon us,
>   even as we hope in you.[8]

Laments

3. The **Community Lament**[9] was sung by the assembled people, protesting and grieving the tragedies and injustices in and the threats to their communities.[10] Community laments consist of the peoples' appeals to God and their confidence that God has or will respond to their appeals. Psalm 12 contains the words of a community lament:

Help, O LORD, for there is no longer anyone who is godly;
>   the faithful have disappeared from humankind.
They utter lies to each other;
>   with flattering lips and a double heart they speak.
May the LORD cut off all flattering lips,
>   the tongue that makes great boasts...
The promises of the LORD are promises that are pure,
silver refined in a furnace on the ground,
>   purified seven times.
You, O LORD, will protect us;
>   you will guard us from this generation forever. (12:1–3, 6–7)

4. The **Individual Lament** was sung by a single voice, and like the Community Lament, appealed to God for deliverance from a threatening life situation.[11] Gunkel points out the typical characteristics of these psalms: "first, the wailing, almost desperate lament and the passionate prayer; then, suddenly, the certainty of deliverance in a jubilant tone."[12] Psalm 6 is an individual lament:

O LORD, do not rebuke me in your anger,
>   or discipline me in your wrath.
Be gracious to me, O LORD, for I am languishing;
>   O LORD, heal me, for my bones are shaking with terror...
Turn, O LORD, save my life;
>   deliver me for the sake of your steadfast love...
Depart from me, all you workers of evil,
>   for the LORD has heard the sound of my weeping.
The LORD has heard my supplication;
>   the LORD accepts my prayer.
All my enemies shall be ashamed and struck with terror;
>   they shall turn back, and in a moment be put to shame.
>   (6:1–2, 4, 8–10)

Like the hymns, lament psalms are a distinctive type of psalm (*Gattung*) because they follow a particular format in their structure. Each is composed of the following elements[13]:

a. an *Invocation*, in which the psalmist cries out to God to hear and listen
b. a *Complaint*, in which the psalmist tells God what is wrong
c. a *Petition*, in which the psalmist tells God what the psalmist wants God to do
d. an *Expression of Trust*, in which the psalmist tells God why he or she knows that God can do what the psalmist asks
e. an *Expression of Praise and Adoration*, in which the psalmist celebrates the goodness and sovereignty of God

In Psalm 6, for example, the elements of the lament are included as follows:

a. Invocation—verses 1–4

"O LORD" occurs in each of these verses

b. Complaint—verses 2–3, 6–7

I am languishing…my bones are shaking with terror (v. 2)
My soul also is struck with terror (v. 3)
I am weary with my moaning;
    every night I flood my bed with tears;
    I drench my couch with my weeping.
My eyes waste away because of grief;
    they grow weak because of all my foes. (vv. 6–7)

c. Petition—verses 1–2, 4–5

Do not rebuke me in your anger,
    or discipline me in your wrath.
Be gracious to me…for I am languishing;
Heal me. (vv. 1–2)

Turn…save my life;
    deliver me for the sake of your steadfast love.
For in death there is no remembrance of you;
    in Sheol who can give you praise? (vv. 4–5)

d. Expression of Trust—verses 8–9

Depart from me, all you workers of evil,
>   for the LORD has heard the sound of my weeping.
The LORD has heard my supplication;
>   the LORD accepts my prayer.

e. Expression of Praise and Adoration—verse 10

All my enemies shall be ashamed and struck with terror;
>   they shall turn back, and in a moment be put to shame.[14]

Minor Types

In addition to the four major types of psalms, we may distinguish a number of minor, but significant, types. These psalms are categorized largely by subject matter rather than by form (*Gattung*). For example, a royal psalm may be a hymn or a lament, but is categorized as a royal psalm because its subject matter is the Israelite king.

1. **Royal psalms** speak of the Lord's provision for the Israelite kings who reigned in Jerusalem during the period of the monarchy (ca. 1000–587 B.C.E.).[15] In Psalm 21, we read:

In your strength the king rejoices, O LORD,
>   and in your help how greatly he exults!
You have given him his heart's desire,
>   and have not withheld the request of his lips. *Selah*...
For the king trusts in the LORD,
>   and through the steadfast love of the Most High he shall not
>   be moved. (21:1–2, 7)

2. **Creation psalms** celebrate God's sovereignty over the created world and the special place of human beings in the world.[16] The words of Psalm 8 sing to us:

O LORD, our Sovereign,
>   how majestic is your name in all the earth!...
When I look at your heavens, the work of your fingers,
>   the moon and the stars that you have established;
what are human beings that you are mindful of them,
>   mortals that you care for them? (8:1, 3–4)

3. **Wisdom psalms** provide instruction in right living and right faith in the tradition of the other wisdom writings of the Old Testament—Proverbs, Ecclesiastes, and Job.[17] In most of these psalms, the

path to wisdom is through adherence to the Torah, the instruction of the Lord. The words of Psalm 1 instruct the reader:

> Happy are those
>> who do not follow the advice of the wicked,
> or take the path that sinners tread,
>> or sit in the seat of scoffers;
> but their delight is in the law of the LORD,
>> and on his law they meditate day and night.
> They are like trees
>> planted by streams of water,
> which yield their fruit in its season,
>> and their leaves do not wither. (1:1–3)

4. **Enthronement psalms** celebrate the enthronement of the Lord as king in the midst of the people of God.[18] As we will see in later chapters, the theme of "the kingship of God" is an important element of the story of the book of Psalms. Psalm 99 proclaims:

> The LORD is king; let the peoples tremble!
>> He sits enthroned upon the cherubim; let the earth quake!
> The LORD is great in Zion;
>> he is exalted over all the peoples.
> Let them praise your great and awesome name.
>> Holy is he!
> Mighty King, lover of justice,
>> you have established equity;
> you have executed justice
>> and righteousness in Jacob. (99:1–4)

See appendix I for a full listing of the psalms in the Hebrew Psalter and their types (*Gattungen*).

Hermann Gunkel's classification of the psalms into particular types has been a lasting legacy, impacting and influencing the study of the Psalter for nearly 100 years.

Setting in Life

In addition to studying the forms of the psalms in the Psalter, Gunkel also puzzled over their origins and asked questions:

• Who composed them? Why?
• Where were they sung? On what occasions?

To answer these questions, Gunkel attempted to describe each psalm's original oral form within the social life of ancient Israel (in German, its *Sitz im Leben*).[19] As we saw in the Introduction, the psalms in the Psalter appear to have come from a variety of times and places in the life of ancient Israel. What we can conclude from outward appearances and from Gunkel's study of form (*Gattung*) and origins (*Sitz im Leben*) is that we have in the Psalter a marvelous mix of psalms, including, among others, the following:

1. Laments, composed and sung by individuals and groups within the family and social life of every period of ancient Israel's history. These laments were handed down generation after generation until they were incorporated into the book of Psalms.
2. Hymns, composed and sung by individuals and groups within the family and social life of every period of ancient Israel's history. These hymns, like the laments, were handed down generation after generation until they were incorporated into the book of Psalms.
3. Psalms developed for specific cultic and royal occasions in the pre-exilic time of ancient Israel's history (before 587 B.C.E.) and recited regularly until they were included in the Psalter.
4. Laments composed on the occasion of specific tragic events in the life of ancient Israel and preserved as a part of the book of Psalms.
5. Psalms written in the postexilic period, many of which may have been written specifically for inclusion in the Psalter.

Preservation and Canonization

How were these Psalms remembered, passed on, and finally included in the Psalter? That is, how did they become a part of the scriptural tradition of the ancient Israelites? The preservation of tradition took place in Israelite communities through a long process of selection and repetition. The process begins when an idea or story (in this case, a psalm) passes what James A. Sanders calls "the immense barrier from a first telling to a second."[20] Someone sings or recites a psalm. Members of the community find in its words help for understanding how to relate to God, and so they sing or recite it again. Someone else finds help in its words, and that person sings it again. The process is repeated over and over until the psalm is firmly entrenched in the minds and hearts of the people. From that time on, it becomes a part of the collected tradition of the community.

But as the psalm is repeated in the community, it changes and updates ever so subtly. When people repeat words, they may be able to do so verbatim. The very fact, however, that the later context of reciting and hearing involves different members of the community in a different time and place—people who bring new questions and concerns to the words of the psalm—gives the psalm a new, sometimes different, meaning. This shift in meaning is crucial to the survival of the psalm. For an idea or a story or a psalm can only cross the barrier from a first telling to a second and a third and a fourth—and thus become tradition—if it is able to meet new needs, to answer questions in new situations. Otherwise it would not continue to be selected, repeated, and preserved by succeeding communities.

Psalm 74 is a good example. It is usually dated to the exilic period of ancient Israel's history (587–538 B.C.E.). The Israelites were in captivity in Babylon; Jerusalem and the temple had been destroyed; and the people called on God to remember the promises which God made to them in former times:

> O God, why do you cast us off forever?
>> Why does your anger smoke against the sheep of your
>> pasture?...
> How long, O God, is the foe to scoff?
>> Is the enemy to revile your name forever?
> Why do you hold back your hand;
>> why do you keep your hand in your bosom?...
> Have regard for your covenant,
>> for the dark places of the land are full of the haunts of
>> violence.
> Do not let the downtrodden be put to shame;
>> let the poor and needy praise your name.
>> (74:1, 10–11, 20–21)

The words of Psalm 74 were most likely recited many times during the exile in Babylon. After the Israelites were allowed to return to Jerusalem in 538, the words would have taken on new meaning as the people contended with one oppressive ruler after another. The foe mentioned in verse 10 changed from the Babylonians to the Greek overlords to the Roman governors. The scoffing changed from scoffing at captives in exile to scoffing at a subservient, inferior people. The dark places of the land conformed to the shape of the landscape whether in Babylon or in Palestine or among the Jewish Diaspora. Still, with the change of context and thus of contents, the words of the lament continued to have meaning, continued to meet needs and answer questions for successive generations of ancient Israelites. Thus Psalm 74 became traditional in the life of the people.

Psalm 23 is perhaps the best-known and best-loved of the psalms in the Psalter.

> The LORD is my shepherd, I shall not want.
>> He makes me lie down in green pastures;
> he leads me beside still waters;
>> he restores my soul…
> You prepare a table before me
>> in the presence of my enemies;
> you anoint my head with oil;
>> my cup overflows…
> And I shall dwell in the house of the LORD
>> my whole life long. (23:1–2, 5–6)

Its imagery is powerful. Yet most of us have never seen a shepherd except on television or in a Christmas play at church. Few of us have been in up-close contact with a sheep, so as to become familiar with its behavior. We have never had our head anointed with oil. Yet, we have appropriated the words, the imagery, and the message of Psalm 23 to our twenty-first-century, largely urban culture so that it is as meaningful to us as to the Israelite psalmist who first uttered its words. Psalm 23 has, indeed, crossed the barrier from a first telling to a second and a third and a fourth. Thus it has become tradition because it has been able to meet new needs and to answer questions about how we are to relate to this God we worship in ever-new situations.

Whatever their origins, types, and reasons for being repeated and handed on, the psalms as we now have them are part of a 150–psalm collection we call the Hebrew Psalter. In the next chapter, we will explore the shape of this book we call Psalms.

3

The Shape of the Psalter

Authorship in the Ancient Near East

When we readers in the twenty-first century talk about literature, one of the first questions we ask is, "Who wrote it?" It matters a great deal to us whether William Shakespeare or René Descartes or John Grisham has written what we are reading. Have the words on the page been penned by a sixteenth-century playwright, a seventeenth-century philosopher, or a twentieth-century novelist? The answer to the question informs somewhat how we analyze and understand what we are reading. It helps us "fill in" the story-world created by the author, to understand the thought-world surrounding the words. But when we talk about literature from the ancient Near East, we are missing the seemingly-important dimension of authorship.

Anonymity

Almost all of the literary works of the ancient Near East that have been discovered are anonymous. They are not signed, and no named authors take credit for them. The great epics from Mesopotamia, such as *Enuma Elish* and *The Epic of Gilgamesh* have no named authors. Egyptian texts such as *The Execration Texts* and *The Tale of Sinuhe* are not attributed to individual writers. The writings from ancient Palestine, such as *The Tale of Aqhat* and *The Balaam Text* from Deir 'Alla, are anonymous.[1] Texts were created and copied and handed down generation after generation within communities with no great concern about the "original" author or "crafter" of the story or text. More importance was attached to the meanings of the stories, the songs, the sets of instructions, or the prophetic words for the community than to the individual writers or the original date of the composition. Yes, authors do bring their own voices to their works. But as the texts are handed on generation after generation, they become more the voices of the communities than the voices of individual writers.

Biblical Attributions

Various books of the Bible, however, are attributed to and even bear the names of individuals in the life of ancient Israel. Jewish and Christian traditions maintain that Moses wrote the Pentateuch and that Samuel and Ezra shaped the Deuteronomistic History (the books of Joshua, Judges, 1 and 2 Samuel, and 1 and 2 Kings). The Psalter is attributed to David and the wisdom books to Solomon. The prophetic books are titled with the individual names of prophets in ancient Israel. But Norman Gottwald reminds us of key differences between biblical times and today:

> The biblical world was surprisingly devoid of personal pride in authorship and it knew nothing of copyright laws. When the Torah or Pentateuch is assigned to Moses, the psalms to David, and wisdom books to Solomon, we should probably understand Moses as the prototype of lawgiver, David as the prototype of psalmist, and Solomon as the prototype of sage or wise man.[2]

Prototype

someone or something that serves as a typical example; a model

---

David was indeed the prototype psalmist. The traditions relating David to songs and song-writing are pervasive in the pages of the Hebrew Bible. 1 Samuel 16; 2 Samuel 1, 22, and 23; 1 Chronicles 16 and, 25; and Amos 6:5 allude to David's song-writing and song-singing.

> Now these are the last words of David:
> The oracle of David, son of Jesse,
>   the oracle of the man whom God exalted,
> the anointed of the God of Jacob,
>   And the sweet psalmist—נְעִים זְמִרוֹת (n^e ʿîm z^{e}mirôt) of
> Israel.[3] (2 Sam. 23:1)

> Alas for those who lie on beds of ivory,
>   and lounge on their couches,
> and eat lambs from the flock,
>   and calves from the stall;

who sing idle songs to the sound of the harp,
>and like David improvise on instruments of music. (Amos
6:4–5)

Several of the Dead Sea Scrolls contain portions of the Psalter. One of them, Psalm Scroll 11QPs[a], contains the following notice:

> And David, the son of Jesse, was wise, and a light like the light of the sun, and literate, and discerning and perfect in all his ways before God and men. And the LORD gave him a discerning and enlightened spirit. And he wrote 3,600 psalms; and songs to sing before the altar over the whole-burnt perpetual offering every day, for all the days of the year, 364; and for the offering of the Sabbaths, 52 songs; and for the offering of the New Moons and for all the Solemn Assemblies and for the Day of Atonement, 30 songs. And all the songs that he spoke were 446, and songs for making music over the stricken, 4. And the total was 4,050. All these he composed through prophecy which was given him from before the Most High.[4]

We read the following in the *Midrash Tehillim,* a rabbinic commentary on Psalms:

> A parable tells us, there was a company of musicians that sought to sing a hymn to the king. The king said to them: To be sure, all of you are sweet singers, all of you are musicians, all of you have superior skill, all of you are men worthy of taking part in the singing of a hymn to the king, yet let the hymn, in whose singing all of you will take part, bear the name of only one man among you because his voice is the sweetest of all your voices. Thus it is written, *The saying of David the son of Jesse…the sweet singer of the Psalms of Israel.*[5]

Scholars' Conclusions

David is strongly connected with song singing in the traditions of ancient Israel. But did David actually write the psalms in the Psalter? The superscriptions of 73 of the 150 psalms in our book of Psalms connect those psalms with David. Many others are connected with persons referred to elsewhere in the biblical text: Moses, Ethan, Korah, Asaph, and Solomon. But we can by no means assign precise authorship or date to any of the psalms in the Hebrew Psalter, for two major reasons.

The Septuagint

a translation of the Hebrew Bible into Greek, undertaken beginning in the third century, B.C.E., by the Jewish community living in Alexandria in Egypt

Superscription

A superscription is a sort of title for a psalm. In our book of Psalms, 119 psalms have superscriptions, and 31 do not. In the Hebrew Bible, the superscription is actually verse 1 of the psalm. In English Bibles, the superscription directly precedes verse 1.
Psalm 3:

מִזְמוֹר לְדָוִד בְּבָרְחוֹ מִפְּנֵי ׳ ׀ אַבְשָׁלוֹם בְּנוֹ׃   1

יְהוָה מָה־רַבּוּ צָרָי רַבִּים קָמִים עָלָי׃   2

רַבִּים אֹמְרִים לְנַפְשִׁי אֵין יְשׁוּעָתָה לּוֹ בֵאלֹהִים סֶלָה׃   3

Psalm 3:
A psalm of David when he fled from Absalom his son.
1 O LORD, how many are my foes. Many are rising against me;
2 many are saying to me, "There is no help for you in God."

First, scholars disagree as to the origin and date of the superscriptions of the psalms. Were they a part of each psalm's original composition or were they added at later times? One compelling reason for assigning the superscriptions to a date later than the composition of the psalms is that many psalm superscriptions in the Hebrew Bible are different from the superscriptions for the same psalms in the Septuagint (LXX).[6]

- In the Hebrew Psalter the superscription of Psalm 24 is: "Of David. A Psalm." In the Septuagint, Psalm 24's superscription is: "A Psalm of David. The One for the Sabbath."
- Psalm 43 has no superscription in the Hebrew Psalter, but in the Septuagint, we find "A Psalm of David" at its beginning.

Second, the nature of the Hebrew language renders impossible a precise translation of the psalm superscriptions. Two examples will suffice.

- A number of psalms are superscripted with the Hebrew words מִזְמֹר לְדָוִד (mizmōr le dāwid), usually translated as "a psalm of

David." The Hebrew word translated "of" is a preposition which actually has a whole range of meanings, including "to, for, at the direction of, of." Thus we may translate these superscriptions as "a psalm for David," "a psalm to David," "a psalm (composed) at the direction of David," or "a psalm of David."

- In the same way, a number of psalms are superscripted לִבְנֵי קֹרַח *(libnê qōrāh)*, usually translated as "of the sons of Korah." Again, the Hebrew word translated "of" can mean "to, for, at the direction of, of." And we may translate these superscriptions as "to the sons of Korah," "for the sons of Korah," "at the direction of the sons of Korah," or "of the sons of Korah."

The inconsistency of superscriptions between the various "versions" of the Hebrew Psalter and the difficulty of translating the Hebrew preposition used frequently in the psalm superscriptions lead to scholarly uncertainty. We cannot state with certainty that David or Korah or Asaph or Solomon or any other individual composed a particular psalm. So what conclusions are we permitted to make?

Collections in the Psalter

The Hebrew Psalter consists of 150 individual psalms that we are able to categorize by type (*Gattung*) and supposed function in the life (*Sitz im Leben*) of ancient Israel.[7] It also consists of a number of collections of psalms that are grouped together in various ways. Some of the collections that have been identified within the Psalter include:

the Davidic Collections	Pss. 3–41; 51–72; 138–145
the Korahite Collections	Pss. 42–49; 84–85; 87–88
the Elohistic Collection	Pss. 42–83
the Asaphite Collection	Pss. 73–83
the Enthronement of God Collection	Pss. 93–100
the Collection of Psalms of Praise	Pss. 103–107
the Collection of Songs of Ascents	Pss. 120–134
the Collection of Hallelujah Psalms	Pss. 111–118; 146–150

Collections of psalms are identified in two major ways:

1. By a common superscription: In Psalms 3–41, for instance, all of the superscriptions read "of David."[8] Psalms 73–83 are attributed to Asaph, and Psalms 120–134 all contain the designation "A Song of Ascents" in their superscriptions.

2. By a common keyword or theme: All of the psalms in the Elohistic Collection consistently refer to God by the name אֱלֹהִים (ʾelōhîm).[9] The Enthronement Psalms celebrate God's kingship over the people of Israel, and each of the Hallelujah Psalms begins or ends with the word "hallelujah"—הַלְלוּ יָהּ (halelû yāh)—which means "praise the Lord."

The Two Names for God

In the Hebrew Scriptures, two names are used for the God of Israel:

אֱלֹהִים   (ʾelōhîm)—translated in our English Bibles as "God"
יְהוָה (yehwāh)—translated in our English Bibles as "LORD."
Often the two names are combined as "the LORD God" (אֱלֹהִים יְהוָה). Scholars posit that a distinction in the use of these names points to different traditions within the text of the Hebrew Scriptures.

Origins of the Collections

How the specific collections of psalms came into existence is lost to the pages of history.[10] We have a few tantalizing pieces of evidence.

- Notice that in the above listing, Psalms 42–49, one of the Korahite collections, and Psalms 73–83, the Asaphite collection, are also part of the Elohistic collection. Thus we may speculate that Psalms 42–49 and Psalms 73–83 were separate collections before becoming a part of the Elohistic collection.

- Psalms 111–118 (Hallelujah Psalms) and Psalms 120–134 (Songs of Ascents) are distinct collections of psalms within Book Five. The collections each have their own themes and emphases, and so we may speculate that they existed separately before becoming a part of Book Five.

We also have some clues about how the psalms were ordered within their collections. One fascinating instance of the purposeful ordering of psalms occurs in the first Davidic collection (Pss. 3–41). In this collection, the majority of the psalms are laments—twenty-four out of the thirty-nine psalms. At Psalm 18, however, an interesting sequence begins:

- Psalm 18, a royal psalm
- Psalm 19, a creation psalm
- Psalm 20, a royal psalm
- Psalm 21, a royal psalm
- Psalm 22, an individual lament
- Psalm 23, an individual hymn of thanksgiving
- Psalm 24, a community hymn

With Psalm 25, the reader is returned to the characteristic lamenting of this collection of psalms. Can we find some rationale for the grouping together of these non-lament psalms with Psalm 22, an individual lament, in the midst of them?

Scholars look for a common thread of words within a group of psalms. In Psalms 3–41, the first Davidic collection, the word יָשַׁע *(yāšaʿ)* (translated in the NRSV in a number of ways, including "help," "salvation" "deliver," and "victory") occurs twenty-six times, with seventeen of those occurrences in Psalms 18, 20, 21, and 22.[11] Following are some examples (emphases author's):

> You have given me the shield of your *salvation*,
> and your right hand has supported me (18:35)

> May we shout for joy over your *victory*…
> Now I know that the LORD will *help* his anointed;
> he will answer him from his holy heaven
> with mighty *victories* by his right hand (20:5, 6)

> My God, my God, why have you forsaken me?
> Why are you so far from *helping* me, from the words of my
> groaning? (22:1)

Two words for "deliver," נָצַל *(nāṣal)* and פָּלַט *(pālaṭ)*, occur ten times in Psalms 18 and 22,[12] and in only seventeen others places in the rest of Book One.

> He *delivered* me from my strong enemy,
> and from those who hated me;
> for they were too mighty for me. (18:17)

Deliver my soul from the sword,
    my life from the power of the dog! (22:20)

The subject matter of Psalm 22, the only lament in this string of psalms, is a plea for God to help—יָשַׁע (*yāša ʿ*)—and to deliver—נָצַל (*nāṣal*)—the psalmist from the dangers surrounding. The repetition of the words in the psalms preceding Psalm 22 establishes a link between them and Psalm 22.

Scholars also look for a common theme running through a group of psalms. As stated above the themes of "safety" and "deliverance" appear to link Psalms 18, 20, 21, and 22. Psalms 22, 23, and 24 are linked by the same themes, but in the case of Psalms 23 and 24, we find that the "safety" and "deliverance" are realized, rather than anticipated. Let's take a closer look at the story.

We begin with a story from the *Midrash Tehellim*. It associates Psalm 22 with David's early life as a shepherd. According to the *Midrash*, David spoke the words of Psalm 22:21, "Save me from the lion's mouth; from the horns of the wild oxen you have rescued me," at a time when he was out tending the flocks and a wild ox threatened him.

Midrash

The Hebrew root of the word is דָּרַשׁ (*dāraš*), which means "to seek out, to search." The Midrash is a commentary on the Hebrew Scriptures, compiled by rabbinic teachers beginning in the early centuries of the Common Era.

The wild ox lifted David in its horns and was about to gore him, but God rescued him by sending a lion which compelled the ox to kneel in homage before the lion, the king of beasts. God then sent a wild gazelle to distract the lion while David escaped.[13] The superscription of Psalm 22, which reads, "according to the deer of the dawn," can also be translated "concerning the deer of the dawn," and might be a reference to the deer-like creature that saved David from the lion and the wild ox. The midrashic story places the psalm in a story-world and gives the reader a concrete situation in the life of David in which to hear the words, "My God, my God, why have you forsaken me?...Strong bulls surround me..."

Psalm 22 contains all of the elements of a psalm of lament[14] (*Invocation, Complaint, Petition, Expression of Trust,* and *Expression of Praise and Adoration*).

Structure of Psalm 22

- INVOCATION (vv. 1–2)
- COMPLAINT (vv. 1–2)
     TRUST (vv. 3–5)
- COMPLAINT (vv. 6–8)
     TRUST (vv. 9–10)
          PETITION (v. 11)
- COMPLAINT (vv. 12–18)
          PETITION (vv. 19–21)
               PRAISE (vv. 22–31)

The reader notices in this psalm a pattern of "complaint/trust," "complaint/trust/petition," "complaint/(trust)/petition/praise." But notice that an *Expression of Trust* is missing from the final progression.

In the psalm following Psalm 22, however, Psalm 23, the psalmist expresses trust in the Lord as the "shepherd" who supplies everything the psalmist needs: green pastures, still waters, right paths, protection, abundant sustenance, and a secure dwelling. Might we read Psalm 23's words of trust as the "missing" *Expression of Trust* of Psalm 22? A common thread of words in the two psalms lends credibility to the idea.

In Psalm 22, God lays the psalmist in "the dust of death" (v. 15), "because" (v. 16),, "a band of evildoers" (v. 16) surround the psalmist. In verses 11 and 19, the psalmist cries out, "But you, O LORD, do not be far from me," "because," (v. 11), "trouble is nearby" (v. 11). In Psalm 23, in contrast, even while walking through "the valley of deep darkness (the valley of the shadow of death)" (v. 4), the psalmist will not fear "evil" (v. 4), "because" (v. 4), "you are with me" (v.4). In fact, the psalmist proclaims that the Lord prepares a table "in front of the ones troubling me" (v. 5).

Psalm 22	Psalm 23
"the dust of **death**" (v. 15)	"The valley of the shadow of **death**" (v. 4)
"a band of **evildoers**" (v. 16)	"**evil**" (v. 4)
"**because**" (v. 16)	"**because**" (v. 4)
"but you, O LORD, do not be **far from me**" (v. 11,19)	"you are **with me**" (v. 4)
"**trouble** is nearby" (v. 11)	"in front of **the ones troubling** me" (v. 5)

In Psalm 22, the psalmist feels surrounded, threatened, and bereft of the "saving deliverance" of God. In Psalm 23, the psalmist is still surrounded and threatened, but God is present and protecting, and for the psalmist, that fact makes all the difference, for "safety" and "deliverance" have been realized.

Psalm 24 is a celebratory community hymn, which opens with the words:

> The earth is the LORD's and all that is in it,
>   the world, and those who live in it;
> for he has founded it on the seas,
>   and established it on the rivers. (24:1, 2)

This psalm was most likely sung as worshipers entered the sanctuary or the temple in Jerusalem during the three great pilgrimage festivals of ancient Israel: the Feasts of Unleavened Bread and Passover, First Fruits (Pentecost), and Tabernacles (or Booths).[15] In the postexilic period, Psalm 24 was included as a celebration of creation in a group of psalms called the *Tamid*, which were read during the daily service at the temple.[16]

Psalm 24 connects with Psalm 19, a creation psalm, and functions as an apt closing for this sequence of psalms. The sequence includes royal psalms celebrating the Lord's safe-keeping and deliverance of the psalmist-king (Pss. 18, 20, and 21); a lament in which the psalmist-king pleads for God to deliver (Ps. 22); an individual hymn expressing trust in the shepherd-God who indeed saves and delivers the psalmist (Ps. 23); and a creation psalm celebrating God's sovereignty over the created world (Ps. 24).[17]

The Five Books of the Psalter

We have identified collections (and collections within collections), linked by superscription or theme and found clues about the ordering of psalms within the collections. Readers also observe that the 150 psalms in the Hebrew Psalter are divided into five books:

- Book One, Psalms 1–41
- Book Two, Psalms 42–72
- Book Three, Psalms 73–89
- Book Four, Psalms 90–106
- Book Five, Psalms 107–150

Each book concludes with a doxology:

Blessed be the LORD, the God of Israel,
  from everlasting to everlasting.
Amen and amen. (41:13)

Blessed be the LORD, the God of Israel,
  who alone does wondrous things.
Blessed be his glorious name forever;
  may his glory fill the whole earth.
Amen and amen. (72:18–19)

Blessed be the LORD forever.
  Amen and amen. (89:52)

Blessed be the LORD, the God of Israel,
  from everlasting to everlasting.
And let all the people say, "Amen."
  Praise the LORD! (106:48)

Let everything that breathes praise the LORD!
  Praise the LORD! (150:6)

The similarities among, especially, the first four doxologies include the following words and phrases:

- Blessed be the LORD
- Amen (which occurs in the Psalter only in the doxologies)
- The God of Israel

The similarities strongly suggest that the doxologies were placed at the ends of the books of the Psalter at the same time, although we have no indication of when this may have taken place.

Nevertheless, the practice of dividing the psalms of the Psalter into five books is an early tradition. The Psalm Scrolls found in the Dead Sea caves are divided into five books, even though the individual psalms included within the scrolls differ from our book of Psalms.[18] The *Septuagint* (LXX), the Greek translation of the Hebrew Bible, also divides the Psalter into five books. The *Midrash Tehellim,* which contains material that dates to as early as the first century B.C.E., states in its commentary on Psalm 1:

As Moses gave five books of laws to Israel, so David gave five Books of Psalms to Israel, the Book of Psalms entitled *Blessed is the man* (Ps. 1:1), the Book entitled *For the leader: Maschil* (Ps. 41:1), the Book, *A Psalm of Asaph* (Ps. 73:1), the Book, *A Prayer of Moses* (Ps. 90:1), and the Book, *Let the redeemed of the Lord say* (Ps. 107:2). Finally, as Moses blessed Israel with the words *Blessed art thou, O Israel* (Deut. 33:29), so David blessed Israel with the words *Blessed is the man.*[19]

More clues that shed light on the shape of the Hebrew Psalter may be found by examining the distribution of psalm types and superscriptions within the book itself. First, with regard to psalm types, scholars have noted a "movement" as one reads through the Psalter from psalms that we call "lament" to psalms that we call "hymn" (or "praise"). The Psalter begins with lament. After the introductory Psalms 1 and 2, the reader encounters a string of eleven laments, broken only by the magnificent creation Psalm 8. The end of the Psalter brings an explosion of praise with Psalms 146–150. And in between, the distribution is as follows:

- In Book One, twenty-four of the forty-one psalms (59 percent) are laments, while eight (20 percent) are hymns.
- In Book Two, twenty of the thirty-one psalms (65 percent) are laments, while six (19 percent) are hymns.
- In Book Three, eight of the seventeen psalms (47 percent) are laments, while six (35 percent) are hymns.
- In Book Four, only four of the seventeen psalms (24 percent) are laments, while five (29 percent) are hymns.
- In Book Five, only ten of the forty-four psalms (23 percent) are laments, while twenty-three (52 percent) are hymns.

Laments dominate the first portion of the Psalter; hymns dominate the second portion.

Second, the superscriptions of the psalms in the Hebrew Psalter may shed some light on the shape of the book. The number of psalms with superscriptions is significantly greater at the beginning of the Psalter than at the end:

- In Book One, thirty-nine of the forty-one psalms have superscriptions (95 percent).
- In Book Two, thirty of the thirty-one psalms have superscriptions (97 percent).
- In Book Three, all seventeen psalms have superscriptions (100 percent).
- In Book Four, only six of the seventeen psalms have superscriptions (35 percent).

- In Book Five, only twenty-six of the forty-four psalms have superscriptions (59 percent).

In the same way, psalms attributed to David are much greater in number in the first portion of the Psalter:

- In Book One, thirty-nine of the forty-one psalms are attributed to David (95 percent).
- In Book Two, eighteen of the thirty-one psalms are attributed to David (58 percent).
- In Book Three, only one of the seventeen psalms is attributed to David (6 percent).
- In Book Four, only two of the seventeen psalms are attributed to David (12 percent).
- In Book Five, fourteen of the forty-four psalms are attributed to David (32 percent).

Each of these phenomena may contribute to our understanding of how the communities of faith who repeated and handed down the psalms of ancient Israel shaped the psalms into the book we call the Hebrew Psalter.

The Compilation Process

- A psalm is composed.
- It is linked with other psalms to form a small collection.
- Small collections are brought together to form larger collections.
- The 150–psalm Hebrew Psalter is formed.

Canonization Summary

In summary, then, the book of Psalms in the Hebrew Bible is a collection of 150 psalms that were organized at some point in their history into small groups, then collections, and then books. The details of that process are lost to the pages of history. But the process began with the words of a single psalm. Someone in ancient Israel sang the psalm, repeated its words, and handed it on. This occurred a second time, and a third—person to person, then generation to generation. Psalm singers took that one psalm and connected it with another and another and another until they had created a collection of psalms. That collection of psalms was recited and handed on, person to person, generation to generation. Gradually, the small collection was grouped with other psalms into a still-larger "collection of collections." That collection of collections was recited and handed on, generation after generation, and was combined with other "collections of collections" until we arrive at the document we call the book of Psalms. In the next chapter, we will examine the history of the people who recited, handed on, and collected the psalms, for perhaps their story will give us some clues about the shape and story of the Hebrew Psalter.

4

The History behind
the Shaping of the Psalter

The individual psalms in the Hebrew Psalter come from many times and many places in the lives of the ancient Israelites, our ancestors in the faith. They were recited, reworked, handed on, joined together, and finally fixed into their canonical shape over a period of some two thousand years. Twenty-first-century readers puzzle over this well-loved book, and they ask questions. One type of question of particular interest to readers during recent years is that of the organization of the book. We ask: Why these 150 psalms? Why are they in this particular order? Why does Psalm 1 come first in the Psalter? Why is Psalm 90 placed at the beginning of Book Four? Why are there more laments at the beginning of the Psalter and more hymns at its end?

Psalms outside the Psalter

The psalms in the Psalter are not the only ones that existed in ancient Israel. The Hebrew Bible itself contains a number of psalms outside the pages of the book of Psalms:

> I called to the LORD out of my distress,
> and he answered me;
> out of the belly of Sheol I cried,
> and you heard my voice…
> As my life was ebbing away,
> I remembered the LORD;
> and my prayer came to you,
> into your holy temple.
> Those who worship vain idols
> forsake their true loyalty.

But I with the voice of thanksgiving
>   will sacrifice to you;
what I have vowed I will pay.
>   Deliverance belongs to the LORD! (Jon. 2:2, 7–9)

My heart exults in the LORD;
>   my strength is exalted in my God.
My mouth derides my enemies,
>   because I rejoice in my victory.
There is no Holy One like the LORD,
>   no one besides you;
>   there is no Rock like our God. (1 Sam. 2:1b–2)

The words of Psalm 105 are duplicated in 1 Chronicles 16:

O give thanks to the LORD, call on his name,
>   make known his deeds among the peoples.
Sing to him, sing praises to him,
>   tell of all his wonderful works...
He is the LORD our God;
>   his judgments are in all the earth.
Remember his covenant forever,
>   the word that he commanded, for a thousand generations,
the covenant that he made with Abraham,
>   his sworn promise to Isaac. (1 Chr. 16:8–9, 14–16 [quoting Ps. 105:1–2, 7–9])

Ordering the Psalms

The type, the *Gattung*, called psalm is not unique to the book of Psalms. But the book itself is a unique collection of psalms. Why these 150 psalms? Why are they in this particular order? We are not the first to ask the question. The *Midrash* on Psalm 3 states:

As to the exact order of David's Psalms, Scripture says elsewhere: *Man knoweth not the order thereof* (Job 28:13). R. Eleazar taught: The sections of Scripture are not arranged in their proper order. For if they were arranged in their proper order, and any man so read them, he would be able to resurrect the dead and perform other miracles. For this reason the proper order of the sections of Scripture is hidden from mortals and is known only to the Holy One, blessed be He, who said, *"Who, as I, can read and declare it, and set it in order?"* (Isa. 44:7).

When R. Joshua ben Levi sought to arrange the Psalms in their proper order, a heavenly voice came forth and commanded: "Do not rouse that which slumbers!"[1]

Perhaps Rabbi ben Levi is wiser than we are, but we will rouse the slumbering book and ask it to shed some light on our questions about its shape and form. And perhaps we will learn from its story.

The book of Psalms most likely did not achieve the "shape" in which we have it in our Old Testament until late in the postexilic period, perhaps as late as the first century of the common era.[2] What do we know about the religious, social, and political situation of the postexilic community, the community that shaped the Psalter into its final 150–psalm format?

The Historical Background behind the Canon of Psalms

The Babylonians and Persians

The last chapters of 2 Kings inform us that in 597 B.C.E., the army of the Babylonian Empire carried King Jehoiachin of Judah, a descendant of David, and many of his subjects into exile (2 Kings 25). A decade later, Babylon's army sacked Jerusalem and destroyed the temple. The nation of Israel had been ruled by the Davidic dynasty for

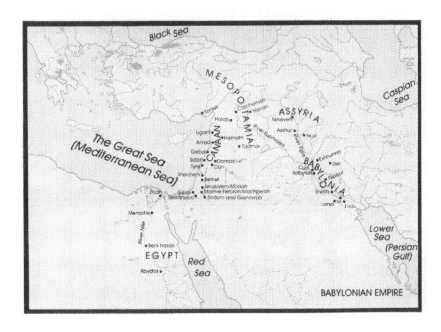

four hundred years. Now the nation was at an end. The dynasty had nothing to rule. Babylon ruled Palestine.

Within fifty years, however, the Babylonian Empire had badly deteriorated. In 539, its capital city fell to Cyrus II, leader of the Persian Empire. In the following year, Cyrus issued an edict that has come to be known, because of its cylindrical shape, as the "Cyrus Cylinder":

> I am Cyrus, the king of the world, great king, legitimate king, king of Babylon, king of Sumer and Akkad, king of the four rims (of the earth), son of Cambyses, great king, king of Anshan, descendant of Teispes, great king, king of Anshan, of a family (which) always (exercised) kingship...(As to the region) from...as far as Ashur and Susa, Agade, Eshnunna, the towns Zamban, Me-Turnu, Der as well as the region of the Gutians, I returned to (these) sacred cities on the other side of the Tigris, the sanctuaries of which have been ruins for a long time, the images which (used) to live therein and established for them permanent sanctuaries. I (also) gathered all their (former) inhabitants and returned (to them) their habitations.[3]

The book of Ezra contains a notice of the same royal edict:

> Thus says King Cyrus of Persia: The LORD, the God of heaven, has given me all the kingdoms of the earth, and he has charged me to build him a house at Jerusalem in Judah. Any of those among you who are of his people—may their God be with them!—are now permitted to go up to Jerusalem in Judah, and rebuild the house of the LORD, the God of Israel—he is the God who is in Jerusalem; and let all survivors, in whatever place they reside, be assisted by the people of their place with silver and gold, with goods and with animals, besides freewill offerings for the house of God in Jerusalem. (Ezra 1:2–4)[4]

Sometime after 538 B.C.E., a group of Jewish exiles made their way from Babylon to Jerusalem to begin the process of rebuilding Jerusalem and the temple.

Persia divided its vast empire into administrative districts called satrapies. Judah was part of the satrapy of *Abar Nahara*—"Beyond the River"—which lay west and south of the Euphrates and included Syria, Phoenicia, Palestine, and Cyprus. Judah appears to have been a distinct unit within the satrapy and was ruled by a separately-appointed governor. Zerubbabel was probably one of those governors.[5] He came to Jerusalem during the reign of Cyrus' son Cambyses (530–522) and was resident there during most of the restoration work on the temple.

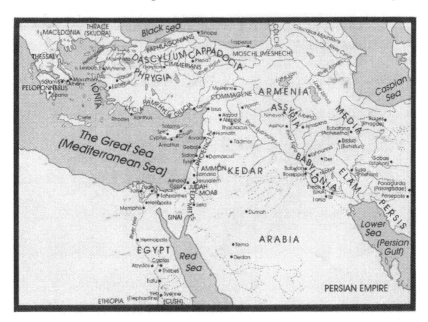

After the death of Cambyses in 522, the Persian Empire experienced turmoil and rebellion in many of its provinces, and Cambyses' successor, Darius I, worked for several years to consolidate his power. Jerusalem may have taken advantage of the turmoil and tried to restore the preexilic Israelite kingdom of David in the person of Zerubbabel. The book of Haggai records the following:

> "On that day", says the LORD of hosts, "I will take you, O Zerubbabel my servant, son of Shealtiel," says the LORD, "and make you like a signet ring, for I have chosen you," says the LORD of hosts. (Hag. 2:23)

The book of Zechariah states the following:

> The hands of Zerubbabel have laid the foundation of this house; his hands shall also complete it…For whoever has despised the day of small things shall rejoice, and shall see the plummet in the hand of Zerubbabel. (Zech. 4:9–10)

Interestingly, Zerubbabel abruptly disappeared from the scene in postexilic Jerusalem sometime around 519.[6] Darius I passed through

Palestine about the same time on his way to put down a rebellion in Egypt, and we may ask: Did the Persians assassinate Zerubbabel? Did they remove him from office and take him into exile? Or did he die coincidentally at that time? Perhaps Zerubbabel had come too close to reestablishing the Davidic monarchy in Jerusalem and had threatened Persia's hold on this geographically-strategic piece of land. Regardless of what happened to Zerubbabel, however, Darius I allowed the Jews to complete the restoration of the temple.

By 515, the temple at Jerusalem was rebuilt and functioning as a cult center:

> And this house was finished on the third day of the month of Adar, in the sixth year of the reign of King Darius. The people of Israel, the priests and the Levites, and the rest of the returned exiles, celebrated the dedication of this house of God with joy. (Ezra 6:15–16)

The Persian Empire allowed the Jewish people to rebuild their temple and resume their religious practices and even to exercise a limited degree of self-rule, but their practices could not interfere with or contradict the laws of the Persian Empire. For the postexilic Israelite population of Judah, that meant that the temple and cult were restored, but the nation-state which had been ruled by the Davidic dynasty was not.

Josephus

Flavius Josephus was a Jewish historian and Roman citizen who lived in the first century, C.E. He was the author of a number of significant works on Jewish life at the time: *The Wars of the Jews, The Antiquities of the Jews,* and *Against Apion.*

The Greeks

At the end of the fourth century B.C.E., a change of power came to Palestine. Alexander the Great conquered the Persian Empire, established Greek rule in Judea, and introduced Hellenistic culture. We actually know very little about Jewish history during the early part of the Hellenistic period, but Josephus' *The Antiquities of the Jews* indicates that Alexander granted Judaism some status as a legitimate religion. He writes that, on an official visit to Jerusalem, Alexander summoned the Jews before him and bade them ask what favors they pleased of him: whereupon the high priest desired that they might enjoy the laws of their forefathers, and might pay no tribute on the seventh year. He granted them all that they desired.[7]

After the untimely death of Alexander in 323 B.C.E., his vast empire was divided among his most powerful generals. Palestine became a sought-after trophy in a power struggle between the Seleucids of Syria and the Ptolemies of Egypt. The Ptolemies held Palestine through most of the third century, but the Seleucid Antiochus III, "the Great," conquered the area in 200 B.C.E. Antiochus III appears to have dealt quite favorably with the Jewish population of Judea. According to Josephus, he issued a decree shortly after conquering Jerusalem:

> Since the Jews, upon our first entrance on their country demonstrated their friendship towards us; and when we came to their city, received us in a splendid manner, and came to meet us with their senate, and gave abundance of provisions to our soldiers...we have thought fit to reward them, and to retrieve the condition of their city...I would also have the work about the temple finished, and the cloisters, and if there be anything else that ought to be rebuilt.[8]

But after the death of Antiochus III, the situation quickly deteriorated. Antiochus's son Antiochus IV "Epiphanes" inaugurated ruthless religious controls in Judea. In 168 B.C.E., he banned circumcision, observance of the Sabbath and holy days, and even the reading of the Torah. In addition, the Jerusalem temple was converted into a pagan sanctuary.[9]

The Jewish Rebellion

The Hellenizing policies finally prompted a rebellion by a group of Jews. Their initial goal was to regain their religious freedom and to restore Jewish worship in the temple. Mattathias, a member of the Hasmonean family, led the first revolt against the Seleucids. The author of the book of 1 Maccabees relates Mattathias's speech to a gathering of Jewish rebels:

> Even if all the nations that live under the rule of the king obey him, and have chosen to obey his commandments, everyone of them abandoning the religion of their ancestors, I and my sons and my brothers will continue to live by the covenant of our

ancestors. Far be it from us to desert the law and the ordinances. We will not obey the king's words by turning aside from our religion to the right hand or to the left. (1 Macc. 2:19–22)

The Jews quickly achieved their goals. In 164 B.C.E., Antiochus V, the son of Antiochus IV, wrote a letter that is preserved in 2 Maccabees:

We have heard that the Jews do not consent to our father's change to Greek customs, but prefer their own way of living and ask that their own customs be allowed them. Accordingly, since we choose that this nation also should be free from disturbance, our decision is that their temple be restored to them and that they shall live according to the customs of their ancestors. (2 Macc. 11:24–25)

The next goal of the Jewish rebels was complete political independence from the Seleucid empire. Only a self-governing nation-state, they deemed, would give them a full restoration of identity and hope for the future. The Hasmoneans obtained Roman support for their endeavor in 161 B.C.E., since Rome was interested in weakening Syrian hold on the East. Josephus quotes the words of the Roman decree:

The decree of the senate concerning a league of assistance and friendship with the nation of the Jews. It shall not be lawful for any that are subject to the Romans to make war with the nation of the Jews, nor to assist those that do so, either by sending them corn, or ships, or money; and if any attack be made upon the Jews, the Romans shall assist them.[10]

The pact with Rome and the growing disintegration of the Seleucid monarchy permitted the Hasmoneans to establish an independent Jewish state by 141 B.C.E. The Hasmoneans, however, were not any more successful at self-rule than their Persian and Greek overlords had been at ruling the empire. The dubious reigns of Alexander Jannaeus (103–76 B.C.E.) and his wife Alexandra Salome (76–67 B.C.E.) marked the end of the Hasmonean dynasty and a short-lived independent Jewish state. The Roman general Pompey conquered Jerusalem in the late autumn of 63 B.C.E. and brought Palestine under the rule of Rome. The years of independence, though short, made a lasting impact on ancient Judaism. The long hoped-for restoration of an Israelite nation proved to be only a passing phenomenon. The world had not been set aright; Judaism was again under the thumb of a foreign power.

An Identity in New Circumstances

The remembered past of the Israelites as a nation with king and court, temple and cult, had to be updated to accommodate the new exigencies of life. The postexilic Jewish people could not have a king of their own. The temple at Jerusalem and the religious practices of the people were permitted, but a nation-state with a Davidic king at its head was not; Israel was a vassal people. Under the same circumstances, many nation-states in the ancient Near East simply disappeared from history. But ancient Israel did not. Through all the turmoil, this people found a new structure for existence and identity that went beyond traditional concepts of nationhood. Temple and cult, rather than king and court, had to be the center of life.

A number of scholars have discussed the way in which Israel went about this restructuring of their existence. Jacob Neusner describes the process as an exercise in which the people were consumed with "an obsessive self-consciousness."[11] James Sanders writes that the people found a "dynamic source of identity."[12] And Walter Brueggemann contends that they engaged in an imaginative process of "world-building."[13] Whether we call it "obsessive self-consciousness," "source of identity," or "world-building," postexilic Israel redefined "nationhood" and found a way to remain a separate and identifiable entity within the vast empires of which it was a part. The postexilic community found a new structure for existence and identity by redefining "nationhood" in the context of its political position within the ancient Near East.

Israel survived because the people asked basic, existential questions of identity and survival—Who are we? Where have we come from? And where are we going? They found answers to the questions in their stories, traditions, and national documents. They appropriated and shaped those oral and written texts into a constitutive document of identity, one that told a story about who they were, where they came from, and where they were going. We call that document the Hebrew Scriptures, our Old Testament. What is the story of the Hebrew Scriptures?

The books of the Pentateuch (Genesis, Exodus, Leviticus, Numbers, and Deuteronomy) tell us that Israel actually became a nation, a clearly identifiable group of people, during the period of the exodus and the wilderness wanderings. During that time, the Israelites had to rely completely on the Lord to provide for, sustain, and protect them. The Lord was their sole source of survival. In Exodus 15 and Deuteronomy 32, Moses sings songs to the Lord and describes the Lord in very kingly language.

"I will sing to the LORD for in triumph he has triumphed,
   The horse and its rider he has thrown into the sea.
   ...the LORD is a man of war, the LORD is his name.
...the LORD will rule forever and ever." (Ex. 15:1, 3, 18, [author's
   translation])

For I proclaim the name of the LORD
   Ascribe greatness to our God.
The Rock! His work is perfect,
   For all His ways are just;
A God of faithfulness and without injustice,
   Righteous and upright is He. (Deut. 32:3, 4, NASB)

In Deuteronomy 33:5, Moses declares that God is king over Israel with
the words, "And he will be in Yishurun (Jerusalem) a king" (author's
translation).

According to the Deuteronomistic Historian, though, the situation
changed after the ancient Israelites settled in the land of Canaan, the
promised land. They demanded that Samuel, the judge and prophet,
anoint a human king for them:

Now appoint a king for us to judge us like all the nations. (1 Sam.
   8:5, NASB)

Samuel was displeased, but the Lord said to him,

Listen to the voice of the people in all that they say to you; for
they have not rejected you, but they have rejected me from being
king over them...Now then, listen to their voice; only—you shall
solemnly warn them, and show them the ways of the king who
shall reign over them. (1 Sam. 8:7, 9)

The next verses of chapter 8 outline for the people the "ways of the
king," but the people reply, "No! but we are determined to have a king
over us, so that we also may be like other nations" (1 Sam. 8: 20).

So Samuel anointed Saul as king over Israel, and from that time
until the Babylonian exile 400 years later, the people had an earthly king
"to judge them," just as the other peoples in the ancient Near East. The
Lord even made a covenant with David, promising that David's throne
would be established forever (2 Sam. 7).

The remainder of the story in the Hebrew Bible is the story of
Israel's disobedience to God, largely through the actions of its kings. Over

and over again in the Books of Kings, we read: "[The king] did what was evil in the sight of the LORD, walking in the way of his ancestor and in the sin that he caused Israel to commit" (1 Kings 15:26, 34; 16:19; 2 Kings 13:2,11; etc.). When the Assyrians destroyed the northern kingdom in 721 B.C.E., the writers of 2 Kings gave this as the reason:

> This occurred because the people of Israel had sinned against the LORD their God who had brought them up out of the land of Egypt from under the hand of Pharaoh king of Egypt. They had worshiped other gods and walked in the customs of the nations whom the LORD drove out before the people of Israel, and in the customs that the kings of Israel had introduced...Jeroboam [the first king of the northern kingdom of Israel] drove Israel from following the LORD and made them commit great sin. The people of Israel continued in all the sins that Jeroboam committed; they did not depart from them until the LORD removed Israel out of his sight. (2 Kings 17:7–8, 21–23)

God preserved the southern kingdom of Judah, "for the sake of my servant David" (1 Kings 11:32; 15:4; etc.). But the reign of Manasseh in the late seventh century B.C.E. marked a turning point in the life of the southern kingdom. Manasseh had led Judah far astray from following after the Lord. According to 2 Kings 21, he erected altars to other gods in the temple, subjected his son to trial by fire, practiced soothsaying and augury, and dealt with mediums and wizards. God spoke to the people about Manasseh:

> Because King Manasseh of Judah has committed these abominations, has done things more wicked than all that the Amorites did, who were before him, and has caused Judah also to sin with his idols; therefore thus says the LORD, I am bringing upon Jerusalem and Judah such evil that the ears of everyone who hears of it will tingle...I will cast off the remnant of my heritage, and give them into the hands of their enemies. (2 Kings 21:11–12, 14)

So in 597, the Babylonians invaded Jerusalem, took King Jehoiachin into exile, and returned ten years later to destroy the city and its temple. Fifty years later, the Persians allowed the Israelites to return to Jerusalem and rebuild the temple. But the Israelites lived from that time on as vassals to the Persians, the Greeks, and then the Romans. King and court were gone, but somehow Israel survived. How?

Remember that an earthly king had not always been a part of Israel's past. At the beginning of Israel's national history God, rather than a human being, ruled over the Israelites. The oral traditions and written texts appropriated and shaped into a constitutive document of identity by the postexilic community recounted the stories of that time in Israel's history, explained how the people had arrived at their current situation, and gave them hope for a continuing existence into the future.

The Psalter was a part of that constitutive document. The postexilic community shaped the cultic materials, the "psalms," of ancient Israel into a popular expression of confidence in a new order, a new statement of national identity. With the surety of the story of the Psalter, ancient Israel could continue to exist as an identifiable entity in a world it no longer controlled.

As we will see in the following chapters, the book of Psalms is shaped into five books which narrate a history of ancient Israel, the very history we read in the books of Samuel, Kings, Chronicles, Ezra, Nehemiah, and a number of the prophets. Books One and Two (Pss. 1–72) celebrate the reigns of Kings David and Solomon; Book Three (Pss. 73–89) laments the dark days of oppression during the divided kingdoms; Book Four recalls the years of the Babylonian exile when the Israelites had to rethink their identity as the people of God (Pss. 90–106); and Book Five (Pss. 107–150) rejoices in Israel's restoration to the land and in the reign of the Lord as king. With the surety of the story of Psalter (and the story found in the rest of the Hebrew Scriptures), the postexilic Israelite community could continue to exist as an identifiable entity in a world it no longer controlled.

In closing the chapter, I quote James Sanders, whose words inspired me many years ago to delve more deeply into the story of this people we call the Israelites:

> Why did Israel survive? That is the immense historical question that begs explanation. That which happened to some of the other victim nations [the Babylonians, the Persians, the Greeks, and the Romans] did not happen to Israel. Israel changed rather radically, to be sure, from being a nation with its own government and a highly nationalist cult, to being a dispersed religious community (whether in Palestine or outside it) called

Judaism. But the point is that Israel survived whereas others did not.[14]

Why did Israel survive? The story of the Psalter helps us we as seek an answer to this vexing question.

5

Book One of the Psalter

Book One of the Psalter consists of two unequal parts:

1. two introductory psalms (Pss. 1 and 2), that, as we will discover, provide the lenses through which readers are instructed to approach the Psalter
2. thirty-nine psalms of David (Pss. 3–41), which commemorate the reign of the great king of ancient Israel

As readers enter Book One, they enter the world of the "golden age" of ancient Israel, when a king of God's choosing reigned in Jerusalem. The chart below indicates each psalm's superscription (if it has one)[1] and the psalm's *Gattung* (type).

Book One	Superscription	Gattung
1	None	Wisdom
2	None	Royal
3	A Psalm of David, when he fled from his son Absalom.	Individual Lament
4	To the leader: with stringed instruments. A Psalm of David.	Individual Lament
5	To the leader: for the flutes. A Psalm of David.	Individual Lament
6	To the leader: with stringed instruments; according to the Sheminith. A Psalm of David.	Individual Lament
7	A Shiggaion of David, which he sang to the LORD concerning Cush, a Benjaminite.	Individual Lament
8	To the leader: according to the Gittith. A Psalm of David.	Creation
9	To the leader: according to Muthlabben. A Psalm of David.	Individual Lament

10	(A Psalm of David)	Individual Lament
11	To the leader. Of David.	Individual Lament
12	To the leader: according to the Sheminith. A Psalm of David.	Community Lament
13	To the leader. A Psalm of David.	Individual Lament
14	To the leader. Of David.	Community Lament
15	A Psalm of David.	Community Hymn
16	A Miktam of David.	Individual Lament
17	A Prayer of David.	Individual Lament
18	To the leader. A Psalm of David the servant of the LORD, who addressed the words of this song to the LORD, on the day when the LORD delivered him from the hand of all his enemies, and from the hand of Saul. He said:	Royal
19	To the leader. A Psalm of David.	Creation
20	To the leader. A Psalm of David.	Royal
21	To the leader. A Psalm of David.	Royal
22	To the leader: according to The Deer of the Dawn. A Psalm of David.	Individual Lament
23	A Psalm of David.	Individual Hymn
24	Of David. A Psalm.	Community Hymn
25	Of David.	Individual Lament
26	Of David.	Individual Lament
27	Of David.	Individual Lament
28	Of David.	Individual Lament
29	A Psalm of David.	Community Hymn
30	A Psalm. A Song at the dedication of the temple. Of David.	Individual Hymn of Thanksgiving
31	To the leader. A Psalm of David.	Individual Lament
32	Of David. A Maskil.	Wisdom
33	(Of David)	Community Hymn
34	Of David, when he feigned madness before Abimelech, so that he drove him out, and he went away.	Individual Hymn of Thanksgiving
35	Of David.	Individual Lament
36	To the leader. Of David, the servant of the LORD.	Individual Lament
37	Of David.	Wisdom
38	A Psalm of David, for the memorial offering.	Individual Lament

39	To the leader: to Jeduthun. A Psalm of David.	Individual Lament
40	To the leader. Of David. A Psalm.	Individual Lament
41	To the leader. A Psalm of David.	Individual Hymn of Thanksgiving

The Introductory Psalms

The first psalm of the Psalter is classified as a "wisdom" psalm, which we define as a psalm that "provides instruction in right living and right faith in the tradition of the other wisdom writings of the Old Testament." The psalm begins "Happy/blessed/content is the one." אַשְׁרֵי הָאִישׁ (*'ašrê hā'îš*)—These wisdom words call the reader to heed the words that follow in order to find happiness or contentment.

> Happy is the one
>> who does not walk in way of the wicked,
> or take the path that sinners tread,
>> or sit in the seat of scoffers.
> But that one's delight is in the law of the LORD,
>> and on his law that one meditates day and night.[2]
> (Ps. 1:1–2, author's translation)

The path to happiness and blessing may be found, according to the psalmist, by diligently adhering to the "law," the "Torah" (תּוֹרָה) of the Lord.

The "Torah" referred to in Psalm 1 is not the "law" that we usually associate with the Hebrew Bible—the set of rules given by God to the Israelites in Exodus and Leviticus. Torah was a positive concept to the author of Psalm 1 and to the community of faith who placed the psalm at the beginning of the Psalter. In its literary sense, the Torah is the whole of the five books of the Pentateuch—the history of ancient Israel as well as the laws given to the people—and a better translation for the word is probably "instruction." The Torah is the ancient Israelites' memory of God's total involvement in their life.

Torah Piety

diligent adherence to the instructions found in the stories, the laws, and the prophetic words of the Torah, the first five books of the Old Testament

---

James L. Mays writes, "*Torah* in Psalm 1 means instruction in the broadest sense, tradition that is authoritative for the people of God."[3] Torah is the central theme of Psalm 1, and adherence to its message (what scholars call "Torah Piety") will prove to be a major theme of the entire Psalter.

According to the words of Psalm 1, meditating upon the Lord's instruction separates the righteous ones—צַדִּיקִים *(ṣᵉdîqîm)*—from the wicked ones—רְשָׁעִים *(rᵉšāᶜîm)*. We encounter the wicked ones in other psalms as the oppressors against whom the psalmists lament.[4] Psalm 1 suggests that the way to overcome the wicked ones is to delight in and meditate on the Torah of the Lord continually. The wicked ones will be driven away like chaff (v. 4), and the righteous ones will be firmly planted, bear fruit, and prosper (v. 3). Psalm 1 does not offer the reader more than one pathway to life. It clearly emphasizes that the only path is "the way of the righteous ones"—דֶּרֶךְ צַדִּיקִים *(derek ṣᵉdîqîm)* (v. 6). Psalm 1 provides a lens, so to speak, through which the rest of the Psalter is to be read and understood. But it is only half the lens; the remainder is found in the following psalm.

Psalm 2 is classified as a Royal psalm.[5] Royal psalms are defined in chapter 2 as those which "speak of the Lord's provision for the Israelite kings who reigned in Jerusalem during the period of the monarchy (ca. 1000–587 B.C.E.)." We may divide Psalm 2 into four sections:

- Verses 1–3 describe conspiracy and plotting by nations, people, kings, and rulers against the Lord and the Lord's anointed. An interesting feature of this section of Psalm 2 is the language the psalmist uses to express the action of the conspirators:

Why do the nations conspire,
  and the peoples *plot* in vain? (2:1)

The word translated "plot" in the second half of verse 1 is from the Hebrew root הָגָה *(hāgāh)*, and is the same word which is translated in Psalm 1, verse 2, as "meditate."

But that one's delight is in the law of the LORD,
  and on his law that one *meditates* (from the root הָגָה *[hāgāh]*)
    day and night. (1:2, author's translation)

The nations, peoples, kings, and rulers in Psalm 2 are clearly distinguished from the righteous ones in Psalm 1. Both are "meditating, musing, mulling over," but for very different purposes.

- In verses 4–6 of Psalm 2, the scene changes to the heavenly realm where the Lord sits enthroned, looking down on the scene below. The psalmist uses powerful anthropomorphic language to describe the Lord's attitude toward those who are conspiring and plotting.

The one who sits in the heavens laughs;
　　the LORD scoffs at them.
Then he will speak to them in his wrath,
　and terrify them in his fury, saying,
"I have set my king on Zion, my holy hill." (2:4–5, author's
　　translation)

The Lord laughs, scoffs, speaks in wrath, and terrifies with fury. The nations, the peoples, the kings, and the rulers who are plotting have no power over the situation. The Lord will place a king of divine choosing on Zion.

- In verses 7–9, the king recites the decree of the Lord:

He said to me, "You are my son;
　　today I have begotten you.
Ask of me, and I will make the nations your heritage,
　　and the ends of the earth your possession." (2:7–8, author's
　　translation)

The words found here might have been spoken at an actual enthronement ceremony in Jerusalem.[6] The decree of the Lord was a document given to the king by the Lord during the king's coronation ceremony. It renewed God's covenant commitment to the dynasty of David and established the nature and authority of the newly-crowned king.[7]

- Some commentators maintain that a key to understanding Psalm 2 is how one chooses to translate verses 11 and 12. The NRSV renders the verses in the following way:

Serve the LORD with fear,
　　with trembling kiss his feet,
or he will be angry, and you will perish in the way.

The New American Standard Bible translates the verses differently:

Worship the LORD with reverence
　　And rejoice with trembling.

Do homage to the Son, that He not become angry, and you
perish in the way.

A textual difficulty in these verses makes it possible to translate the
words at the end of verse 11 and the beginning of verse 12 as either
"with trembling kiss his feet" or "rejoice with trembling, do
homage to the Son."[8] Regardless of the translation one chooses,
however, the impact of the psalm is the same. The psalmist exhorts
the hearer to "serve the LORD," "with fear and trembling." If God
has chosen an earthly king to occupy the throne in Jerusalem, then
a measure of that "service," "fear," and "trembling" is to be given to
the king.

- Psalm 2 ends in verse 12b with the words "Happy—יֵרְשַׁא
  (ʾašrê)—are all who take refuge in him"—words which echo the
  opening line of Psalm 1, "Happy—יֵרְשַׁא (ʾašrê)—is the one
  who…"

Psalms 1 and 2 are the only untitled psalms in Book One of the
Psalter. The remainder of the psalms in the book, Psalms 3–41, are
identified in their superscriptions as "psalms of David."[9] As we saw in
chapter 3, untitled psalms are rare in Books One, Two, and Three of the
Psalter. When they occur, we must pay attention. Untitled psalms appear
to have been used at various junctures in these books as introductions
and as transitions from one collection of psalms to another.[10] Psalms 1
and 2 may be read as an introduction to the story of the Psalter. Psalm
1 urges the reader to meditate upon the Torah as the path to right living,
and Psalm 2 states that, regardless of the useless plotting of earthly rulers,
the God who sits in the heavens is sovereign over the created order.
These, then, are the two lenses through which the reader is to view the
Psalter. J. Clinton McCann summarizes the message of Psalms 1 and 2:
"The entire Psalter will be about the 'happy'/'blessed' life, and it will
affirm throughout that this life derives fundamentally from the
conviction that God rules the world."[11]

The First Davidic Collection

Psalm 3 begins an extended collection of "psalms of David," in
which the reader encounters David in all facets of his life: David the
king and David the human being, with all his victories and strengths, all
his shortcomings and flaws.[12] We read David's heartfelt laments:

O LORD, how many are my foes!
Many are rising against me;

many are saying to me,
    "There is no help for you in God." (3:1–2)

How long, O LORD? Will you forget me forever?
    How long will you hide your face from me?
How long must I bear pain in my soul
    and have sorrow in my heart all day long?
How long will my enemy be exalted over me? (13:1–2)

We read David's equally stirring praises:

I love you, O LORD, my strength.
The LORD is my rock and my fortress and my deliverer,
    my God, my rock, in whom I take refuge;
    my shield and the horn of my salvation, my stronghold.
    (18:1–2)

Rejoice in the LORD, O you righteous.
    Praise befits the upright.
Praise the LORD with the lyre;
    make melody to him with the harp of ten strings.
Sing to him a new song;
    play skillfully on the strings, with loud shouts.
For the word of the LORD is upright,
    and all his work is done in faithfulness. (33:1–4)

We read of David's awe of the God who created the world and
humankind:

When I look at your heavens, the work of your fingers,
    the moon and the stars that you have established;
what are human beings that you are mindful of them,
    mortals that you care for them?
Yet you have made them a little lower than God,
    and crowned them with glory and honor. (8:3–5)

The heavens are telling of the glory of God;
    and the firmament proclaims his handiwork. (19:1)

Psalm 3

After the two introductory psalms, Psalm 3 stands at the beginning
of the collection of psalms of David. It is an individual lament, which
we defined in chapter 3 as "an individual appeal to God for deliverance
from a threatening life situation." Twenty-three of the psalms in Book

One are laments, and Psalm 3 is a good model for the kinds of psalms the reader will encounter in this book of the Psalter. Its superscription reads, "A Psalm of David, when he fled from his son Absalom" (see 2 Sam. 15–17). Twelve other psalms in the Psalter locate themselves, in their superscriptions, in particular historical settings in the life of David: Pss. 7, 18, 34, 51, 52, 54, 56, 57, 59, 60, 63, and 142.

With the opening of Psalm 3, the reader is taken into the very midst of the life of David, the celebrated king of ancient Israel. David represents the golden age of the nation of Israel, the days of a kingdom that stretched "from Dan to Beersheba." But the superscription of Psalm 3 reminds the reader that David's reign was not all that it might have been. It was marked by deceit (Uriah and Bathsheba—2 Sam. 11–12); violence (Amnon and Tamar—2 Sam. 13); intrigue (Amnon and Absalom—2 Sam. 13); and outright revolt (Absalom—2 Sam. 14–18). James L. Mays writes:

> David was the sweet psalmist of Israel. The songs that came out of his life as shepherd and warrior, as refugee and ruler, were the inspired expression of a life devoted to God in bad times and good, and therefore the guiding language for all who undertook lives of devotion.[13]

The five elements of the lament psalm are found in Psalm 3 as follows:

1. the Invocation:
O LORD (vv. 1, 3, 7)
O my God (v. 7)

2. the Complaint:
How many are my foes!
   Many are rising against me;
many are saying to me,
   "There is no help for you in God." (vv. 1–2)

3. the Petition:
Rise up, Deliver me! (v. 7)

4. the Expression of Trust:
But you, O LORD, are a shield around me,
   my glory, and one who lifts up my head.
I cry aloud to the LORD,
   and he answers me from his holy hill.
I lie down and sleep;

I wake again, for the LORD sustains me.
I am not afraid of ten thousands of people
 who have set themselves against me all around...
For you strike all my enemies on the cheek;
 you break the teeth of the wicked. (vv. 3–7)

5. the expression of praise:
Deliverance belongs to the LORD;
 may your blessing be on your people! (v. 8)

Psalm 3 is a simple psalm of lament and a powerful introduction to the collection of psalms in Book One. Using the paradigm of the life of David, the Lord's chosen king, the psalm begins in distress. Enemies are all around and are talking together about the psalmist. But the psalmist is confident that the Lord will deliver because the Lord has delivered in the past. Because of that, the psalmist can lie down and sleep without fear of the multitudes that surround. Psalm 3 contains words of confidence sung by David, words of confidence to be heeded by the reader of the psalm. Despite the circumstances, one has only to rely on the Lord as David did, and God will "strike all the enemies on the cheek and break the teeth of the wicked" and bless the people.

Psalm 8

Twenty-three of the remaining thirty-eight psalms in Book One are laments of David. The first non-lament psalm the reader encounters in this David collection is Psalm 8, which is classified as a creation psalm, a psalm which celebrates God's sovereignty over the created world and the special place of human beings in the world. We may outline it in the following way:

- Verses 1–2 celebrate the majesty of the Lord, and though full of textual difficulties, state that God rules over and will silence the enemy and the avenger.
- Verses 3–4 describe humanity's sense of insignificance in the face of the moon and stars in God's heavens.
- Verses 5–8 express humanity's sense of awe at its God-given role in creation.
- Verse 9 repeats the words of verse 1 as a concluding praise of the majesty of the Lord.

Within the words, the verses, and the structure of the psalm, the reader encounters a masterful composition.

Verse 1a and 9:

O LORD, our Sovereign, how majestic is your name in all the earth.

יְהוָה אֲדֹנֵינוּ מָה־אַדִּיר שִׁמְךָ בְּכָל־הָאָרֶץ

Verse 1b:

You have set your glory above the heavens.

אֲשֶׁר תְּנָה הוֹדְךָ עַל־הַשָּׁמָיִם:

The word translated "our Sovereign"—אֲדֹנֵינוּ (ᵃdōnênû) is a common way to address a king in the Hebrew Bible and in other literature in the Ancient Near East, and the word translated "your glory"—הוֹדְךָ (hôdᵉkā) is a word often used to refer to the king's glory. The beginning and ending of Psalm 8, then, reiterates the message of Psalm 2: The Lord, the God of Israel, reigns over "all the earth."

In verse 2 of Psalm 8, the psalmist emphasizes that God will silence the enemy and the avenger, just as the psalmist in Psalm 3 was confident that God would strike the enemies "on the cheek" and "break the teeth of the wicked" (3:7).

In verse 4 of Psalm 8, we read:

What are human beings that you are mindful of them, mortals that you care for them?

מָה־אֱנוֹשׁ כִּי־תִזְכְּרֶנּוּ וּבֶן־אָדָם כִּי תִפְקְדֶנּוּ:

The words translated "human beings" and "mortals" are אֱנוֹשׁ (ᵉnôš) and בֶן אָדָם (ben 'ādām), words that might be read literally as "man" and "son of man" and emphasize our utter humanness in contrast to the divine nature of God. The psalmist questions God's concern for humanity.

A close look at the structure of Psalm 8 gives the reader some clue as to how the psalmist's questioning will be answered. In verses 1 and 9, the psalmist addresses the Lord in two ways, first with the divine name, יְהוָה (yᵉhwāh), translated in our English Bibles as "the LORD," and then with the appellative "our Sovereign." The psalmist continues with the interrogative מָה (māh), translated in verses 1 and 9 as "how": "O LORD, our Sovereign, how majestic..."

In verse 4, the psalmist begins with מָה (māh), the same interrogative pronoun used in verses 1 and 9. In verse 4, though, it is translated as "what," rather than "how," and follows with two names for human beings—אֱנוֹשׁ (ʾᵉnôš) and בֶּן אָדָם (ben ʾādām): "What are human beings...what are mortals." But the Hebrew word is the same.

The use of מָה (māh) and two designations for the subjects in each of the verses alert the reader to a purposeful connection between verses 1, 4, and 9. Psalm 8 certainly contrasts the sovereignty of God with the earthliness of humanity, but the two are inextricably connected.

Verse 1

יְהוָה אֲדֹנֵינוּ מָה

O LORD, our Sovereign, how...

Verse 4

מָה אֱנוֹשׁ...וּבֶן אָדָם

what are human beings...and mortals...

Verse 9

יְהוָה אֲדֹנֵינוּ מָה

O LORD, our Sovereign, how...

Verse 5 states that God has made humanity a little lower than אֱלֹהִים (ʾᵉlōhîm), a word which may be translated as "God," "gods," or even "divine beings." Verse 6 says that God has given humanity "dominion over" or more literally, "you have caused him to rule over" the works of God's hands. God has made humanity only a little lower than God's self and God has given them the task of "ruling" (as a king would rule) over the created world. Thus we see God engaging humanity in a kind of partnership in the care of creation. Peter Craigie summarizes the message of Psalm 8: "Though the universe is vast and imparts to humankind a sense of smallness and insignificance, nevertheless God has given to humankind a position of extraordinary strength within the universe."[14]

A Return to Laments

Psalm 9 returns the reader to the characteristic lamenting of Book One of the Psalter. Psalms 9–14 and 16–17 are laments. Psalm 18, like Psalm 2, is a royal psalm. Like Psalm 3, its superscription gives it a specific setting in the life of David: "A Psalm of David the servant of the

LORD, who addressed the words of this song to the LORD on the day when the LORD delivered him from the hand of all his enemies, and from the hand of Saul."

Psalm 19

Psalm 19, another creation psalm, begins with words that echo the beginning of Psalm 8:

> The heavens are telling the glory of God,
>   and the firmament proclaims his handiwork.
> Day to day pours forth speech,
>   and night to night declares knowledge. (19:1–2)

> O LORD, our Sovereign,
>   how majestic is your name in all the earth!
> You have set your glory above the heavens. (8:1)

But Psalm 19 adds a new element to the celebration of the Lord's creation work: the Torah and its accompanying attributes.

> The law [Torah] of the LORD is perfect,
>   reviving the soul;
> the decrees of the LORD are sure,
>   making wise the simple;
> the precepts of the LORD are right,
>   rejoicing the heart;
> the commandment of the LORD is clear,
>   enlightening the eyes;
> the fear of the LORD is pure,
>   enduring forever;
> the ordinances of the LORD are true
>   and righteous altogether. (19:7–9)

Because of its many references to the Torah, a number of commentators categorize Psalm 19 as a "Torah" psalm, rather than as a creation psalm. James L. Mays defines Torah psalms as "psalms in which the instruction of the Lord is the central organizing topic and is viewed as the primary reality in the relations of mortals to God."[15] The reader of the psalms must always keep in mind that the *Gattungen*, the types, of the psalms, are later literary categories laid down over psalms whose writers had no idea that they were composing "lament psalms," "royal psalms," "wisdom psalms," or "creation psalms." The ancient Israelite composers of the psalms were expressing themselves out of the depths of their experience and had no idea that literary critics 2,500 years later would categorize their compositions into fixed, analyzed forms.

Psalm 19 may, therefore, be viewed by modern scholars as a Torah psalm; but Psalm 19 *is* a song of creation. Psalm 19 joins the created world celebrated in Psalm 8 with the Torah, the divine instruction given by God to the Israelites during the wilderness wanderings. Creation and Torah are thus joined together as the Lord's works and words to the reader of the Psalter. The created order praises God and the Torah enables humankind to maintain the goodness of the created order.

The End of Book One: Psalm 41

In chapter 3, we undertook a detailed study of Psalms 18–24, so we will not comment any further about them here, except to remind the reader that these psalms (with the exception of Psalm 22) are an extended interruption of the characteristic lamenting of Book One of the Psalter.

In Psalm 25, the reader is returned to lamenting, broken only occasionally by hymns (Pss. 29, 30, 33, 34) and by wisdom psalms (Pss. 32, 37). Book One does not end in lamenting, though. Psalm 41 is categorized as an Individual Hymn of Thanksgiving, defined in chapter 2 as "a single voice praising God for goodness to or on behalf of that individual, usually deliverance from some trying situation." The psalm expresses great self-assurance that the Lord is gracious to and pleased with the psalmist:

> By this I know that you are pleased with me;
>> because my enemy has not triumphed over me.
> But you have upheld me because of my integrity,
>> and set me in your presence forever. (41:11–12)

A collection that begins in lament ends with a hymn praising God for God's goodness to the psalmist. But the reader has encountered such praise over and over again in Book One, since each psalm of lament includes an expression of praise as part of its intrinsic form. We may read Psalm 41, then, as an extended reiteration of the expressions of praise that the psalmists sing at the conclusion of all of the laments.

Interestingly, Psalm 41 begins with the same word with which Psalm 1 begins and Psalm 2 ends, "happy"—אַשְׁרֵי *('ašrê)*, forming an inclusio around the entirety of Book One.

> Happy are those who consider the poor [or weak];
>> the LORD delivers them in the day of trouble. (41:1)

The inclusio reminds the reader who has arrived at the end of Book One that happiness is found in observance of the Torah (Torah Piety) and that one aspect of that observance is to consider (and the Hebrew word here actually means "to be wise about"—from the root שָׂכַל [*śākal*]) the "weak," those less able than others to care for themselves.

Book One ends with a doxology (a closing word of praise), as does each book of the Psalter:

> Blessed by the LORD, the God of Israel,
>> from everlasting to everlasting.
> Amen and Amen. (41:13)

Summary

Book One introduces the two themes of the book of Psalms, Torah piety and the kingship of the Lord. It goes on to tell the story of the life of King David. David sang songs of lament and praise, gave voice to hymns of wonder at the creator God, and celebrated the goodness of God to God's chosen ruler. The reader has been drawn into the world of the monarchy of ancient Israel. The psalms that follow will lead the reader through the remainder of the days of King David.

6

Book Two of the Psalter

Book Two of the Psalter continues the story of the reign of King David. But other actors enter the stage. Psalms of the Korahites and Asaphites, priestly singers during the reigns of David and Solomon, occur at the beginning of the book. A lamenting David appears in the heart of the book, and it ends with a royal psalm ascribed to Solomon, which we may read as the blessings of David upon his son and successor, Solomon. David's reign comes to an end, and the kingdom is placed in the hands of the descendants of the king chosen by God to rule over the nation of Israel. Book Two consists of Psalms 42–72. The chart below indicates each psalm's superscription (if it has one)[1] and the psalm's *Gattung* (type).

Book Two	Superscription	Gattung
42	To the leader. A Maskil of the Korahites.	Individual Lament
43	(a Maskil of the Korahites)	Individual Lament
44	To the leader. Of the Korahites. A Maskil.	Community Lament
45	To the leader: according to Lilies. Of the Korahites. A love song.	Royal
46	To the leader. Of the Korahites. According to Alamoth. A Song.	Community Hymn
47	To the leader. Of the Korahites. A Psalm.	Enthronement
48	A Song. A Psalm of the Korahites.	Community Hymn
49	To the leader. Of the Korahites. A Psalm.	Wisdom
50	A Psalm of Asaph.	Community Hymn

51	To the leader. A Psalm of David, when the prophet Nathan came to him, after he had gone in to Bathsheba.	Individual Lament
52	To the leader. A Maskil of David, when Doeg the Edomite came to Saul and said to him, "David has come to the house of Ahimelech."	Individual Lament
53	To the leader: according to Mahalath. A Maskil of David.	Community Lament
54	To the leader: with stringed instruments. A Maskil of David, when the Ziphites went and told Saul, "David is in hiding among us."	Individual Lament
55	To the leader: with stringed instruments. A Maskil of David.	Individual Lament
56	To the leader: according to The Dove on Far-off Terebinths. Of David. A Miktam, when the Philistines seized him in Gath.	Individual Lament
57	To the leader: Do Not Destroy. Of David. A Miktam, when he fled from Saul, in the cave.	Individual Lament
58	To the leader: Do Not Destroy. Of David. A Miktam.	Community Lament
59	To the leader: Do Not Destroy. Of David. A Miktam, when Saul ordered his house to be watched in order to kill him.	Individual Lament
60	To the leader: according to the Lily of the Covenant. A Miktam of David; for instruction; when he struggled with Aram-naharaim and with Aram-zobah, and when Joab on his return killed twelve thousand Edomites in the Valley of Salt.	Community Lament
61	To the leader: with stringed instruments. Of David.	Individual Lament
62	To the leader: according to Jeduthun. A Psalm of David.	Individual Lament
63	A Psalm of David, when he was in the Wilderness of Judah.	Individual Lament
64	To the leader. A Psalm of David.	Individual Lament
65	To the leader. A Psalm of David. A Song.	Creation
66	To the leader. A Song. A Psalm.	Individual Hymn of Thanksgiving
67	To the leader: with stringed instruments. A Psalm. A Song.	Community Hymn
68	To the leader. Of David. A Psalm. A Song.	Community Hymn
69	To the leader: according to Lilies. Of David.	Individual Lament
70	To the leader, Of David, for the memorial offering.	Individual Lament
71	None	Individual Lament
72	Of Solomon.	Royal

The Beginning of Book Two

Book Two begins with a collection of psalms of the Sons of Korah (Pss. 42–49, 84–85, and 87–88) and marks the beginning of what is known as the Elohistic Psalter (Ps. 42–83).[2] Like Book One, Book Two consists mainly of laments (twenty out of thirty-one psalms: 65 percent), but unlike Book One, only eighteen psalms are attributed to David (58 percent).

Psalm 42

Psalm 42, with which the Book opens, is "a Maskil of the Korahites." According to 1 Chronicles, the Korahites were temple keepers and temple singers during the reigns of David and Solomon:

> These are the men whom David put in charge of the service of song in the house of the LORD, after the ark came to rest there. They ministered with song before the tabernacle of the tent of meeting, until Solomon had built the house of the LORD in Jerusalem; and they performed their service in due order. These are the men who served; and their sons were: Of the Kohathites: Heman, the singer, son of Joel, son of Samuel, son of Elkanah, son of Jeroham...son of Tahath, son of Assir, son of Ebiasaph, son of Korah. (1 Chr. 6:31–37)

> Shallum son of Kore, son of Ebiasaph, son of Korah, and his kindred of his ancestral house, the Korahites, were in charge of the work of the service, guardians of the thresholds of the tent, as their ancestors had been in charge of the camp of the LORD, guardians of the entrance. (1 Chr. 9:19)[3]

Psalm 42 is an individual lament in two sections, verses 1–4 and verse 6–10, each followed by the refrain:

> Why are you cast down, O my soul [being—נֶפֶשׁ *(nepeš)*]
> and why are you disquieted within me?
> Hope in God, for I shall again praise him,
> my help and my God. (Ps. 42:5, 11)

Because in Psalm 42, the psalmist is in dialogue with self—נֶפֶשׁ *(nepeš)*—the psalm is often likened to a third-millennium B.C.E. (First Intermediate Period) Egyptian tale called "The Dispute between a Man and His Ba." Miriam Lichtheim, in *Ancient Egyptian Literature*, summarizes the tale:

A man who suffers from life longs for death. Angered by his complaints, his *ba*—וֶפֶשׁ *(nepeš)*—threatens to leave him. This threat fills the man with horror, for to be abandoned by his *ba* would mean total annihilation, instead of the resurrection and immortal bliss that he envisages. He therefore implores his *ba* to remain with him, and not to oppose him in his longing for death.[4]

In a similar way in Psalm 42, the psalmist persuades the being—נֶפֶשׁ *(nepeš)*—not to despair, since the psalmist is convinced that the Lord is still a source of help.

Verses 1–4 and 6–10 use powerful water images to express the psalmist's need for the Lord and the feeling of removal from the Lord's presence.[5] Verses 1–4 are nostalgic, lamenting that life is no longer as it used to be. Thus the psalmist thirsts after brooks of water, cries tears, and pours out the being while remembering:

> How I went with the throng,
>> and led them in procession to the house of God,
> with glad shouts and songs of thanksgiving,
>> a multitude keeping festival. (42:4)

Verses 6–10 use water images to express distress and despair over present circumstances. The psalmist despairs at feelings of being overcome by the deep, by waterfalls, by breakers, and by waves:

> My soul [being] is bowed down within me...
> Deep calls to deep
> at the thunder [voice] of your cataracts;
> All your waves and your billows have gone over me. (vv. 6–7)

The taunts of the psalmist's enemies and adversaries in verses 3 and 10 serve to heighten the psalmist's sense of God's absence and the psalmist's nostalgia.

> My tears have been my food day and night,
> while people say to me continually,
>> "Where is your God?" (v. 3)

> As with a deadly wound in my body,
>> my adversaries taunt me,
> while they say to me continually,
>> "Where is your God?" (v. 10)

Thus God's absence is felt all the more because of the constant reminders from the psalmist's adversaries that God is not "here," is not present. But before feelings of despair completely consume the psalmist, the refrain calls the being back from its musings, reflecting the psalmist's confidence and hope that God is present, even in apparently difficult circumstances. And so the reader enters Book Two of the Psalter with a measure of despair in the midst of current situations, but with an equal measure of hope in God in the midst of difficulty:

> Hope in God, for I shall again praise him,
>> my help and my God. (42:11)

Psalms 43–49: of the Korahites

Because Psalm 43 has the same refrain (in v. 5) as Psalm 42, many argue that the two psalms belong together as a unit.[6] The refrain certainly provides justification for considering the two psalms together. In Psalm 42, however, the psalmist is speaking to self, to נֶפֶשׁ *(nepeš)*, while in Psalm 43 the psalmist is speaking to God. The common refrain may have prompted the collectors of the songs of the Korahites to place these similar psalms side by side, but it does not necessarily indicate that they were at one time a single psalm.

Psalms 43–49, all psalms of the Korahites, are an interesting mix of psalmic *Gattungen*: individual lament, community lament,[7] royal psalm, community hymn, enthronement psalm, and wisdom psalm.

Psalm 50: of Asaph

Psalm 50, a Community Hymn, is, according to its superscription, a psalm of Asaph. Asaph was one of a guild of singers and musicians who, along with the Korahites, served at the temple in Jerusalem during the reigns of David and Solomon. We read in 2 Chronicles that after Solomon had completed the work on the temple and the ark of the covenant had been put in its place in the holy of holies:

> When the priests came out of the holy place (for all the priests who were present had sanctified themselves without regard to their divisions), and all the levitical singers, Asaph, Heman, and Jeduthun, their sons and kindred, arrayed in fine linen, with cymbals, harps, and lyres, stood east of the altar with one hundred twenty priests blowing trumpets, then the trumpeters and singers made themselves heard in unison in praise and thanksgiving to the LORD. (2 Chr. 5:11–13, author's translation)

While there is no evidence that Psalm 50 was used at Solomon's dedication of the temple, which is described in 2 Chronicles 5–7 and 1 Kings 8,[8] its words are apt:

> The mighty one, God the LORD,
>   speaks and summons the earth
>   from the rising of the sun to its setting.
> Out of Zion, the perfection of beauty,
>   God shines forth. (Ps. 50:1–2)

The Heart of Book Two

Psalms 51–65: of David

Beginning with Psalm 51, the reader encounters fifteen psalms of David (Pss. 51–65), eight of which are connected, in their superscriptions, with specific events in the life of David. As with Psalm 3 (see chapter 5), the events recalled in these psalmic superscriptions are not great events of kingly triumph and splendor, but events that depict a very human King David.

Psalm 51: when Nathan the prophet came to him, after he had gone in to Bathsheba (2 Sam. 12:1–15).

Psalm 52: when Doeg the Edomite came and told Saul, and said to him, "David has come to the house of Ahimelech" (1 Sam. 22:6–10).

Psalm 54: when the Ziphites went and told Saul, "David is hiding among us" (1 Sam. 23:15–21).

Psalm 56: when the Philistines seized him in Gath (1 Sam. 21:10–22:1).

Psalm 57: when he fled from Saul, in the cave (1 Sam. 22:1; 24:1–3).

Psalm 59: when Saul ordered his house to be watched in order to kill him (1 Sam. 19:11–17).

Psalm 60: when he struggled with Aram-naharaim and with Aram-zobah, and when Joab on his return killed twelve thousand Edomites in the Valley of Salt (2 Sam. 8).

Psalm 63: when he was in the wilderness of Judah (1 Sam. 22:1–2; 24:1–7).

Many scholars dismiss most of the psalmic superscriptions, particularly the thirteen that link the psalms to specific events in the life

of David, as late additions which offer little in the way of helping readers
to understand the psalms. Brevard Childs, for example, maintains that
the most important factor in the formation of these superscriptions
appears to be not precise references in the psalms to events in David's
life, but "general parallels between the situations described in the psalms
and some incidents in the life of David." He writes further, "The psalms
are transmitted as the sacred psalms of David, but they testify to all the
common troubles and joys of ordinary human life in which all persons
participate."[9] Thus these psalms need not be read in light of the stories
about David to which they refer. As late additions, the superscriptions
may be ignored in our modern context of interpretation.

Not all scholars agree.[10] James Sanders maintains that the editors of
the Psalter purposefully drew attention to very specific events in the life
of David, situations with which they expected their readers to be
familiar. He writes:

> Does not such editorial work indicate the intense interest of
> redactors in date lines and historical contexts? They seem to be
> saying fairly clearly, if the reader wants to understand the full
> import for his or her (later) situation of what Scripture is saying,
> he or she had best consider the original historical context in
> which this passage scored its point.[11]

Therefore, according to Sanders, the superscriptions *do* matter, especially
in the case of those thirteen psalms that refer to specific events in the
life of David. The superscriptions call readers to go back and review the
stories and think about the characters and emotions, the actions and the
outcomes. Then, when readers return to the psalms, they are able to ask
themselves, "How do the psalms express the emotions and outcomes of
the characters and events of those stories?"

Patrick Miller writes this about Psalm 51, whose superscription is:
"To the leader. A Psalm of David, when the prophet Nathan came to
him, after he had gone in to Bathsheba."

> The superscription does not force one to confine the power of
> those words to that occasion alone, but it does illustrate the
> power where such words of passionate self-condemnation and
> extreme plea for transformation and cleansing are appropriate.
> The setting of that psalm against the context of the taking of
> Bathsheba by David is certainly not without justification in the
> light of what one actually encounters in the psalm.[12]

In 2 Samuel 12, when the prophet Nathan confronts David with the implications of what he has done with Bathsheba, David's only words are, "I have sinned against the LORD" (2 Sam. 12:13). Might we read Psalm 51 as the rest of David's words, David's confession of sin and his plea for forgiveness?

> Have mercy on me, O God,
>> according to your steadfast love;
> according to your abundant mercy
>> blot out my transgressions...
> For I know my transgressions,
>> and my sin is ever before me.
> Against you, you alone, have I sinned,
>> and done what is evil in your sight,
> so that you are justified in your sentence
>> and blameless when you pass judgment...
> The sacrifice acceptable to God is a broken spirit;
>> a broken and contrite heart, O God, you will not despise. (Ps. 51:1, 3–4, 17)

Psalm 65: a Creation Psalm

Psalm 65 is the third creation psalm in the Hebrew Psalter. Verses 1–5 praise the God of Zion who answers (v. 2), forgives (v.3), and delivers (v. 5) the people. Verses 6–11 recount the creating and sustaining power of God in the world by means of a plethora of active verbs:

- you establish... (v. 6)
- you silence... (v. 7)
- you awe... (v. 8)
- you make...shout for joy (v. 8)
- you visit... (v. 9)
- you provide... (v. 9)
- you water... (v. 10)
- you crown... (v. 11)
- you cause to overflow... (v. 11)

The closing verses of the psalm narrate how creation reacts to the sustaining God:

> The pastures of the wilderness overflow,
>> the hills gird themselves with joy,
> the meadows clothe themselves with flocks,

> the valleys deck themselves with grain,
>> they shout and sing together for joy. (65:12–13)

Psalms 66–68: Words of Praise

Psalms 66–68 are individual hymns of thanksgiving and community hymns that continue the praise offered to God in Psalm 65.

> Say to God, "How awesome are your deeds!
>> Because of your great power, your enemies cringe before you.
> All the earth worships you;
>> they sing praises to you,
>> sing praises to your name. (66:3–4)

> The earth has yielded its increase;
>> God, our God, has blessed us;
> May God continue to bless us;
>> let all the ends of the earth revere him. (67:6–7)

> Ascribe power to God,
>> whose majesty is over Israel,
>> and whose power is in the skies. (68:34)

Psalm 69: the Lamenting David

With Psalm 69, the reader again encounters the laments of David which are characteristic of Books One and Two of the Psalter. Psalm 69 recalls the water imagery of Psalm 42:

> Save me, O God,
>> for the waters have come up to my neck.
> I sink in deep mire,
>> where there is no foothold;
> I have come into deep waters,
>> and the flood sweeps over me.
> I am weary with my crying;
>> my throat is parched.
> My eyes grow dim
>> with waiting for my God. (69:1–3)

But it ends with the same praise that the reader encountered in Psalms 65–68:

> Let heaven and earth praise him,
>> the seas and everything that moves in them.

> For God will save Zion
>> and rebuild the cities of Judah;
> and his servants shall live there and possess it;
>> the children of his servants shall inherit it,
>> and those who love his name shall live in it. (69:34–36)

The End of Book Two

Psalm 71

Psalm 71 is the only psalm in Book Two without a superscription. It is classified as an individual lament and is subtitled in a number of Bible translations and commentaries as "the prayer of an old man."[13] In verses 6–9 we read:

> Upon you I have leaned from my birth;
>> it was you who took me from my mother's womb.
> My praise is continually of you.
> I have been like a portent to many,
>> but you are my strong refuge.
> My mouth is filled with your praise,
>> and with your glory all day long.
> Do not cast me off in the time of old age;
>> do not forsake me when my strength is spent.

and in verses 17–18:

> O God, from my youth you have taught me,
>> and I still proclaim your wondrous deeds.
> So even to old age and gray hairs,
>> O God, do not forsake me,
> until I proclaim your might
>> to all the generations to come.

As we saw in chapter 5, untitled psalms were used at various places in Books One, Two, and Three of the Psalter as introductions to collections of psalms and as transitions from one collection to another. The untitled "prayer of an old man" moves the reader from Book One's and Book Two's psalms of David to what follows.

Psalm 72: of Solomon

Psalm 72 is a psalm "of Solomon," one of only two psalms in the Hebrew Psalter ascribed to Solomon.[14] It is categorized as a royal psalm, and H.-J. Kraus describes it as a collection of wishes and prayers for the well-being of the king, likely used at a royal enthronement ceremony in Jerusalem.[15] Brevard Childs maintains that the placement of Psalm 72 within the "story" of the Psalter indicates strongly that the psalm "is 'for Solomon,' offered by David."[16] Gerald Wilson concludes the following:

> the clear intent of the heading is to associate Solomon in some fashion with the vision of enduring kingship articulated in the psalm. The traditional connection with Solomon is perhaps seen as a response to the reference in 72:1 to the "king [David?]" and the "royal son [Solomon?]." In addition, the petitionary tone of the psalm seeking righteousness and enduring rule for the king has some resonance with the tone of Solomon's prayer for wisdom and righteous rule in 1 Kings 3:6–15.[17]

Thus we read:

> Give the king your justice, O God,
>   and your righteousness to a king's son.
> May he judge your people with righteousness,
>   and your poor with justice.
> May the mountains yield prosperity for the people,
>   and the hills, in righteousness.
> May he defend the cause of the poor of the people,
>   give deliverance to the needy,
>   and crush the oppressor. (72:1–4)

The Doxology and Closing Verse

Book Two ends with the expected doxology:

> Blessed be the LORD, the God of Israel,
>   who alone does wondrous things.
> Blessed be his glorious name forever;
>   may his glory fill the whole earth.
>   Amen and Amen. (72:18–19)

But the book has an additional ending:

> The prayers of David son of Jesse are ended. (72:20)

David, whose prayers are now ended, moves into the background. Solomon ascends the throne of the nation of Israel. But the splendor of Solomon's kingdom will be short-lived. His son and successor Rehoboam will have the northern half of the country taken from his control by Jeroboam, son of Nebat. Centuries of tension between the kindred nations will ensue, until the northern kingdom is overpowered by the Assyrians in 721 B.C.E. The southern kingdom of Judah will survive for another 130 years, but it too will succumb to the onslaught of a foreign power, Babylon. Book Three of the Psalter recounts the troubled times of the divided kingdoms of Israel.

7

Book Three of the Psalter

The psalms in Book Three of the Psalter reflect events that took place during the period of the divided kingdoms of ancient Israel, the subsequent obliteration of the northern kingdom in 722 by the Assyrians, and, finally, the destruction of the southern kingdom by the Babylonians in 586. When the reader reaches the end of Book Three, the nation of Israel, with a Davidic king at its head, is no more. The book consists of Psalms 73–89. It is short (only seventeen psalms make up this book) and it is heartfelt. Psalms of the community—both hymns and laments—dominate the book. And it ends in the despair of exile. The chart below indicates each psalm's superscription (if it has one)[1] and the psalm's *Gattung*.

Book Three	Superscription	Gattung
73	A Psalm of Asaph.	Wisdom
74	A Maskil of Asaph.	Community Lament
75	To the leader: Do Not Destroy. A Psalm of Asaph. A Song.	Community Hymn
76	To the leader: with stringed instruments. A Psalm of Asaph. A Song.	Community Hymn
77	To the leader: according to Jeduthun. Of Asaph. A Psalm.	Individual Lament
78	A Maskil of Asaph.	Wisdom
79	A Psalm of Asaph.	Community Lament
80	To the leader: on Lilies, a Covenant. Of Asaph. A Psalm.	Community Lament
81	To the leader: according to The Gittith. Of Asaph.	Community Hymn
82	A Psalm of Asaph.	Community Hymn
83	A Song. A Psalm of Asaph.	Community Lament

84	To the leader: according to the Gittith. Of the Korahites. A Psalm.	Individual Hymn of Thanskgiving
85	To the leader. Of the Korahites. A Psalm.	Community Lament
86	A Prayer of David.	Individual Lament
87	Of the Korahites. A Psalm. A Song.	Individual Hymn of Thanksgiving
88	A Song. A Psalm of the Korahites. To the leader: according to Mahalath Leannoth. A Maskil of Heman the Ezrahite.	Individual Lament
89	A Maskil of Ethan the Ezrahite.	Royal

Book Three of the Psalter is dominated by psalms of Asaph, the Korahites, and other singers and musicians who, according to the books of Chronicles, served at the Jerusalem temple during the reigns of David and Solomon (see 1 Chr. 6:31–37; 9:19; and 2 Chr. 15:11–13). David is noticeably absent in Book Three. Only Psalm 86, an individual lament, is attributed to him.

Psalm 73

The first psalm the reader encounters in Book Three is a wisdom psalm of Asaph. Psalm 73 stands in interesting contrast to Psalm 42, the psalm which opens Book Two. In Psalm 42, an Individual Lament, the psalmist feels far away from God (42:1–2), and adversaries taunt the psalmist with the words, "Where is your God?" (42:3, 10). The psalmist debates with the psalmist's being over whether to despair or to hope (42:5, 11). In Psalm 73, however, the psalmist speaks directly to God and expresses a strong sense of nearness to God (73:23–28).

> I am continually with you;
> > you hold my right hand.
> You guide me with your counsel,
> > and afterward you will receive me with honor. (73:23–24)

But though the psalmist is near to God, all still is not well.

> I saw the prosperity of the wicked.
> For they have no pain,
> > their bodies are sound and sleek.
> They are not in trouble as others are;
> > they are not plagued like other people...
> They scoff and speak with malice;

loftily they threaten oppression.
They set their mouths against heaven,
  and their tongues range over the earth…
Such are the wicked;
  always at ease, they increase in riches.
All in vain have I kept my heart clean
  and washed my hands in innocence.
For all day long I have been plagued,
  and am punished every morning. (73:3–5, 8–9, 12–14)

Unlike the orderly world that the reader encounters in Psalm 1, where the wicked—רְשָׁעִים (rᵉšāᶜîm)—are punished and the righteous—צַדִּיקִים (ṣᵉdîqîm)—are rewarded, the singer of Psalm 73 looks at the world around and observes the wicked prospering while the righteous suffer.[2] There seems to be no reasoned connection between righteousness and reward and wickedness and punishment. What has happened to the ordered world of the wisdom teachers?

Humankind in the Ancient Near East believed in a basic moral governance of the universe. Act and consequence were connected in daily life—good followed on good; evil followed on evil; wisdom followed on wisdom; and foolishness followed on foolishness. The book of Proverbs reminds us with its adages:

Whoever walks in integrity walks securely,
  but whoever follows perverse ways will be found out. (10:9)

The wise woman builds her house,
  but the foolish tears it down with her own hands. (14:1)

A fool despises a parent's instruction,
  but the one who heeds admonition is prudent. (15:5)

And recall the words of Psalm 1:

The wicked will not stand in the judgment,
  nor sinners in the congregation of the righteous;
for the LORD watches over the way of the righteous,
  but the way of the wicked will perish. (1:5–6)

Sages and wisdom writers taught that there was a fundamental order in the world which could be discerned by experience, that the gods (or God) had established the order, and that all of humankind—and all of creation—was bound by that order.[3] But Psalm 73, along with other biblical wisdom compositions such as the books of Job and Ecclesiastes, addresses the realities of day-to-day living. In these works, the writers point out that reward does not always come to the righteous or punishment to the wicked, that wisdom does not always come to the prudent or folly to the foolish. Rather, the wicked prosper and the righteous suffer. Job complained:

> Why do the wicked live on,
>> reach old age, and grow mighty in power?...
> Their houses are safe from fear,
>> and no rod of God is upon them....
> They sing to the tambourine and the lyre,
>> and rejoice to the sound of the pipe.
> They spend their days in prosperity.
>> and in peace they go down to Sheol. (Job 21:7, 9, 12–13)

Sheol

"Sheol" comes from a Hebrew word which means "to be extinguished." During most of ancient Israel's history, Sheol was the abode of the dead, somewhere in the depths of the earth, the place where everyone went after life, whether they were righteous or wicked.

The sage of the book of Ecclesiastes wrote the following:

> In my vain life I have seen everything; there are righteous people who perish in their righteousness, and there are wicked people who prolong their life in their evildoing. (Eccl. 7:15)

The ancient Israelites were not the only people to question the conventional wisdom teachings of the ancient Near East. *The Eloquent Peasant* is a story from early second-millennium B.C.E. Egypt in which a peasant is unjustly arrested and imprisoned. Fascinated with the rhetoric the man uses to declare his innocence, the pharaoh orders that the man be held simply to amuse the pharaoh with his speeches. The words of the eloquent peasant sound much like those of the singer of Psalm 73:

> Goodness is destroyed, none adhere to it,
>> In order to fling falsehood's back to the ground.
> If the ferry is grounded, wherewith does one cross?[4]

The compositions *I Will Praise the Lord of Wisdom* and *The Babylonian Theodicy*, from late second-millennium B.C.E. Mesopotamia, also deal with the issue of the wicked prospering and the righteous suffering.

> What is good in one's sight is evil for a god.
> What is bad in one's own kind is good for his god.
> Who can understand the counsel of the gods in the midst of heaven?
> The plan of a god is deep waters; who can comprehend it?[5]

After witnessing the prosperity, the pride, the violence, and the scoffing of the wicked, the singer of Psalm 73 questions whether righteousness is worthwhile.

> All in vain have I kept my heart clean
> and washed my hands in innocence. (Ps. 73:13)

The psalmist is tempted to believe that one who obeys the instructions of the Lord receives no benefit, that faithfulness is "vain," or "emptiness" (the Hebrew word used here comes from root רִיק *[rîq]* which means "to empty" or "to pour out").

The turning point in Psalm 73, though, comes in verses 15–17:

> If I had said, "I will talk on in this way,"
> I would have been untrue to the circle of your children.
> But when I thought how to understand this,
> it seemed to me a wearisome task,
> until I went into the sanctuary of God;
> then I perceived their end. (73:15–17)

The psalmist's remembrance of belonging, of being part of a community, provides the assurance needed not to follow the way of the wicked but to continue to seek righteousness. This sense of community is solidified in the sanctuary where the psalmist experiences the nearness and presence of God.

> When my being was embittered,
> when I was pricked in the heart,
> I was stupid and ignorant;
> I was like a brute beast toward you.
> Nevertheless I am continually with you;
> you hold my right hand.
> You guide me with your counsel,
> and afterward you will receive me with honor. (73:21–24)

Walter Brueggemann writes:

> The old troublesome issues of "conduct and consequence" established in the categories of Psalm 1 are not resolved. Those issues are rather left behind for a greater good. No judgment is finally made whether the world is morally coherent or not, whether Psalm 1 is true or not. It is enough that the God of long-term fidelity is present, caring, powerful, and attentive.[6]

Psalm 74: A Community Lament

Book Three of the Psalter continues with Psalm 74, a Maskil of Asaph, a community lament. Community laments and community hymns are abundant in Book Three—six community laments and three community hymns in the seventeen psalms of the Book. Psalm 74 expresses the community's distress at the same kinds of problems faced by the individual in Psalm 73. In verses 1–11, the psalmist describes the desecration of the sanctuary of the Lord by enemies.

> O God, why do you cast us off forever?
>> Why does your anger smoke against the sheep of your
>> pasture?...
> Your foes have roared within your holy place;
>> they set up their emblems there. (vv. 1, 4)

In verses 18–23, the psalmist calls upon God to remember and act on behalf of the people.

> Remember this, O LORD, how the enemy scoffs,
>> and an impious people reviles your name...
> Have regard for your covenant,
>> for the dark places of the land are full of the haunts of
>> violence. (vv. 18, 20)

The middle portion of the psalm, verses 12–17, provides the rationale for why the psalmist knows that the faithful community can call upon God and expect God to act, forming that part of the lament we call The Expression of Trust.

> Yet God my king is from of old,
>> working salvation in the earth.
> You divided the sea by your might;
>> you broke the heads of the dragons in the waters...
> Yours is the day, yours also the night;

you established the luminaries and the sun.
You have fixed all the bounds of the earth;
    you made summer and winter. (vv. 12–13, 16–17)

Psalm 74's Expression of Trust is a trust in the God who creates and sustains the world. It echoes the sentiments of the creation psalms the reader encountered in Book One's Psalms 8 and 19 and Book Two's Psalm 65.

Psalm 78

Psalms 75–85 are laments and hymns of Asaph and the Korahites.[7] The only interruption in the series is the lengthy Psalm 78, another wisdom psalm. Its subject matter, however, is very different from that of the wisdom psalm (Ps. 73) with which the book opens. Psalm 78 bases its words of wisdom on the history of God's dealings with the ancient Israelites. Samuel Terrien writes about the psalm: "Partly influenced by wisdom poetry, the poet recites, with prolixity and redundancy, a legendary history of Israel, from the Exodus to David."[8] Note its beginning:

Give ear, O my people, to my teachings;
    incline your ears to the words of my mouth.
I will open my mouth in a parable;
    I will utter dark sayings from of old. (vv. 1–2)

Deuteronomistic History

The books of Deuteronomy, Joshua, Judges, Samuel, and Kings are known as the Deuteronomistic History, so called because the theological viewpoint of the book of Deuteronomy informs the viewpoint of the remainder of the books. In each of them, God judges the kings and the people by a single criterion: Have the kings and the people followed the instructions of the Torah and worshiped only the Lord? That is, have they practiced Torah Piety?

The psalm goes on to recount the activity of God in the lives of the Israelites, the story told in the Deuteronomistic History of the Hebrew Scriptures.

(God) established a decree in Jacob,
    and appointed an instruction in Israel,

which he commanded our ancestors
>   to teach to their children. (v. 5)

In the sight of their ancestors [God] worked marvels
>   in the land of Egypt, in the fields of Zoan.
He divided the sea and let them pass through it,
>   and made the waters stand like a heap. (vv. 12–13)

[God] rained down on them manna to eat,
>   and gave them the grain of heaven.
Mortals ate of the bread of angels;
>   he sent them food in abundance. (vv. 24–25)

He led them in safety, so that they were not afraid;
>   but the sea overwhelmed their enemies.
And he brought them to his holy hill,
>   to the mountain that his right hand had won. (vv. 53–54)

He drove out nations before them;
>   he apportioned them for a possession
>   and settled the tribes of Israel in their tents. (vv. 55)

But Psalm 78 also records Israel's distrust of and rebellion against the Lord.

They tested God in their heart
>   by demanding the food they craved.
They spoke against God, saying,
>   "Can God spread a table in the wilderness?" (vv. 18–19)

Yet they tested the Most High God,
>   and rebelled against him.
>   They did not observe his decrees,
but turned away and were faithless like their ancestors;
>   they twisted a treacherous bow. (vv. 56–57)

As a result, the final verses of Psalm 78 tell us:

He rejected the tent of Joseph,
>   he did not choose the tribe of Ephraim;
but he chose the tribe of Judah,
>   Mount Zion, which he loves. (vv. 67–68)

He chose his servant David,
>   and took him from the sheepfolds;

> from tending the nursing ewes he brought him
> to be the shepherd of his people Jacob,
> of Israel, of his inheritance. (vv. 70–71)

The story of Psalm 78 ends with God rejecting the northern tribes of Israel and choosing David's kingdom of Judah "to be the shepherd of his people Jacob" (v. 71). God has not forsaken all of Israel. Judah remains—alone (see 2 Kings 17).

Psalm 86: a Prayer of David

After the group of laments and hymns in Psalms 75–85, the reader comes to Psalm 86, the only psalm in Book Three attributed to David. It is, not surprisingly, an individual lament, described in the superscription as a "prayer"—תְּפִלָּה *(t^epillāh)*—of David. Many scholars have puzzled over the inclusion of this one psalm of David in the midst of a collection of psalms of Asaph, the Korahites, and other temple singers.

The words and phrases used in Psalm 86 are words and phrases the reader encounters in a number of other places in the Hebrew Scriptures, particularly in the Psalter:

- verse 1 in Psalms 40:17; 69:29; 109:22
  Incline your ear, O LORD, and answer me,
  for I am poor and needy.

- verse 4 in Psalms 25:1; 143:8
  Gladden the being of your servant,
  for to you, O LORD, I lift up my being.

- verse 11 in Psalms 27:11; 143:8
  Teach me your way, O LORD,
  that I may walk in your truth;

- verse 14 in Psalm 54:3
  O God, the insolent rise up against me;
  a band of ruffians seeks my life,
  and they do not set you before them.

- verses 5 and 15 in Exodus 34:6[9]
  But you, O Lord, are a God merciful and gracious,
  slow to anger and abounding in steadfast love and
  faithfulness.

One early twentieth-century commentator describes the psalm as "a mosaic of fragments from other Psalms and scriptures," and then goes on to say, "It claims no poetic originality, yet it possesses a pathetic earnestness and tender grace of its own."[10] A commentator in the mid-twentieth century adds these words:

> We are not justified in regarding the affinity of the psalm with other songs as the result of borrowing from other literature in order to mask the author's own incompetence. On the contrary, here we are dealing with a liturgical style which is deliberately used to incorporate the personal concern of the worshipper in the larger context of the worship of the cult community and the speech-forms and thought-forms proper to it.[11]

Echoes of the Past

A number of psalms in the Psalter are made up of echoes, phrases, and even whole verses from other psalms. For example:

- Psalm 26 echoes Psalms 7, 15, 17, 24, and 25.
- Psalm 70 quotes directly from 40:13–17.
- Psalm 71 includes phrases found in Psalms 22, 31, and 70.
- Psalm 78 shares much of the language of Psalm 96.
- Psalm 108 joins together Psalms 57:7–11 and 60:5–12.[12]

This phenomenon suggests that a word or idea that was meaningful for one psalmist in a particular context was found to be meaningful by another in a different context. Appropriated from other psalms and scriptures, the words of Psalm 86 perhaps lent additional significance to the psalmist's message in the context of Book Three's community laments and hymns. By using words and phrases found often on the lips of all the people, this lament of David, the individual worshiper, is incorporated into the worship of the whole community of faith.

> Turn to me and be gracious to me;
> > give your strength to your servant;
> > save the child of your serving girl.
> Show me a sign of your favor,
> > so that those who hate me may see it and be put to shame,
> > because you, LORD, have helped me and comforted me.
> > (86:16–17)

Psalm 88: A Lament

Psalm 88 is the only psalm in the Psalter attributed to Heman the Ezrahite, who served as a singer at the Jerusalem temple. First Kings uses a group of renowned wise persons including Heman and Ethan (to whom Ps. 89 is attributed) to show that Solomon was the wisest of the wise (1 Kings 4:31). Psalm 88 is an individual lament, but a lament like no other in the Psalter since it contains only three of the five elements of a lament psalm.[13] It includes only the *Invocation,* the *Complaint,* and the *Petition,* and omits any *Expression of Trust* and any *Expression of Praise and Adoration.* Even this observation does not fully disclose the unique structure of Psalm 88. The three existing components of a lament are represented very unevenly in the psalm. The *Invocation* and the *Petition* constitute only a very small portion of the psalm:

• the *Invocation*

O LORD, God of my salvation (v. 1)

O LORD (vv. 9, 13, 14)

• the *Petition*

Let my prayer come before you; incline your ear to my cry. (v. 2)

• the *Complaint* consumes the remainder of the psalm:

my being is full of troubles (v. 3)

you have put me in the depths of the Pit (v. 6)

I am shut in so that I cannot escape (v. 8)

 my eye grows dim through sorrow (v. 9)

I suffer your terrors; I am desperate (v. 15)

In addition, the psalmist asks questions of God:

Do you work wonders for the dead?
Do the shades rise up to praise you? (v. 10)

Is your steadfast love declared in the grave,
or your faithfulness in Abaddon? (v. 11)

Are your wonders known in the darkness,
or your saving help in the land of forgetfulness? (v. 12)

O LORD, why do you cast me off?
Why do you hide your face from me? (v. 14)

Psalm 89: a Royal Lament

The complaints and questions of this dark lament are not answered in its verses. The beginnings of an answer may be found in Psalm 89 which follows. We might understand Psalm 89 as a companion to Psalm 88, meant to be read along with it. Psalm 88 is "a maskil[14] of Heman the Ezrahite"; Psalm 89 is "a maskil of Ethan the Ezrahite." It begins with the words:

> I will sing of your steadfast love, O LORD, forever;
>> with my mouth I will proclaim your faithfulness to all
>> generations. (v. 1)

It continues:

> You said, "I have made a covenant with my chosen one,
>> I have sworn to my servant David:
> 'I will establish your descendants forever,
>> and build your throne for all generations.'" (vv. 3–4)

Verses 1–37 of Psalm 89 read much like the other royal psalms the reader has encountered thus far in the Psalter (Pss. 2, 18, 20, 21, 45, and 72). God the creator and ruler of the heavens and the earth chose a kingly family to be God's monarchic family on the earth:

> "I have set the crown on one who is mighty,
>> I have exalted one chosen from the people.
> I have found my servant David;
>> with my holy oil I have anointed him;
> my hand shall always remain with him;
>> my arm also shall strengthen him." (vv. 19–21)

And God promised that the family of David would always rule:

> "Once and for all I have sworn by my holiness;
>> I will not lie to David,
> His line shall continue forever,
>> and his throne endure before me like the sun.
> It shall be established forever like the moon,
>> an enduring witness in the skies." (vv. 35–37)

The tone of Psalm 89 changes dramatically in verse 38. Without explanation, without transition, the royal psalm becomes a lament:

> But now you have spurned and rejected him;
>   you are full of wrath against your anointed.
> You have renounced the covenant with your servant;
>   you have defiled his crown in the dust. (vv. 38–39)

And the questioning of Psalm 88 is taken up once again:

> How long, O LORD? Will you hide yourself forever?
>   How long will your wrath burn like fire?
> Who can live and never see death?
>   Who can escape the power of Sheol?
> Lord, where is your steadfast love of old,
>   which by your faithfulness you swore to David?
>   (vv. 46, 48, 49)

The psalm ends with a plea to God to remember God's servant, and just as with Psalm 88, the lament portion of Psalm 89 has no *Expression of Trust* and no *Expression of Praise and Adoration*.

Royal Psalms

The inclusion of royal psalms such as Psalm 89 at various places in the book of Psalms has puzzled scholars over the years. Except for Psalms 18, 20, and 21, they are not grouped together in a collection; they don't share a common superscription; and in a number of instances, they occur at the beginnings and endings of distinct collections of psalms in Books One, Two, and Three:

- Psalm 2, before Book One's collection of psalms of David;
- Psalm 72, at the end of Book Two; and
- Psalm 89, at the end of Book Three.

The exception to the pattern outlined above is the end of Book One. Psalm 41 is not a royal psalm, although it is a psalm of David. Gerald Wilson provides a plausible explanation:

> An explanation for the absence of a royal psalm at the end of Book One is to recognize that the redactional movement to combine Books One and Two into a single Davidic collection (a movement marked by the postscript in Ps. 72.20, 'The prayers of David son of Jesse are ended') had already taken place when these royal psalms were set in their present positions. As a result,

we are left with two major blocks of material (Pss. 2–72; 73–89) which are marked at the 'seams' by royal psalms.[15]

The End of Book Three

Book Three closes with a terse doxology, the shortest in the Psalter (compare Ps. 41:13; 72:18–19; and 106:48):

Blessed be the LORD forever.
Amen and Amen. (89:52)

Book Three closes with words of lament, in which the psalmist mourns Israel's broken covenant with David and bemoans the taunting of its neighbors. Israel is in exile in Babylon; a foreign power is ruling over them. What hope do they have of survival in the situation? Book Four will admonish the Israelites to look back and remember the time in their past when, not an earthly king, but the Lord their God was sovereign over them—and was their sole means of survival. During the time of the exodus from Egypt and the wilderness wandering, the Lord provided for, protected, and sustained the people. And God can again be provider, protector, and sustainer; but the people must go back, must remember, and must learn from the past. With that knowledge, Israel will be able to survive as a distinct group of people within the vast empires which will conquer them time and again in the centuries following.[16]

8

Book Four of the Psalter

Book Four of the Psalter features two major characters, Moses and God.[1] At this juncture in the story of the Psalter, the Israelites are in exile in Babylon; Jerusalem and the temple are destroyed; and the only hope of survival in these bewildering circumstances is for the people to go back—to remember—a time in their past when God, not an earthly king, was sovereign over them. With the words of Psalm 90, Moses calls the people to remember the exodus from Egypt and the wilderness wandering. This was the time in the life of ancient Israel when the people had to rely completely on their God, Yahweh, to provide for, protect, and sustain them. The exile in Babylon was a new wilderness, and the means of survival was to once again rely completely on Yahweh. Book Four consists of Psalms 90–106. The chart below indicates each psalm's superscription (if it has one)[2] and the psalm's *Gattung*.

Book Four	Superscription	Gattung
90	A Prayer of Moses, the man of God.	Community Lament
91	None	Individual Hymn of Thanksgiving
92	A Psalm. A Song for the Sabbath Day.	Individual Hymn of Thanksgiving
93	None	Enthronement
94	None	Individual Lament
95	None	Enthronement
96	None	Enthronement
97	None	Enthronement
98	A Psalm.	Enthronement
99	None	Enthronement
100	A Psalm of Thanksgiving.	Community Hymn

101	Of David. A Psalm.	Royal
102	A prayer of one afflicted, when faint and pleading before the LORD.	Individual Lament
103	Of David.	Individual Hymn of Thanksgiving
104	None	Creation
105	None	Community Hymn
106	None	Community Lament

One of the first things the reader notices about Book Four is the number of untitled psalms included in it. Ten of its seventeen psalms have no superscriptions. Of the remaining seven, Psalm 90 is attributed to Moses; two psalms (Pss. 101 and 103) are ascribed to David; and four psalms (Pss. 92, 98, 100, and 102) have superscriptions without making connections with an individual or group. Unlike Books One, Two, and Three, psalms of lament do not dominate in Book Four. Of the seventeen psalms in the book, only four are laments (Pss. 90, 94, 102, and 106), while the remaining thirteen are hymnic (Pss. 91, 92, 100, 103, and 105), royal (Ps. 101), creation (Ps. 104), and enthronement (Pss. 93, 95, 96, 97, 98, and 99) psalms.

Psalm 90: A Prayer of Moses

The Book opens with "A Prayer of Moses, the man of God." It is the only psalm in the Hebrew Psalter so designated and is a community lament:

> Lord, you have been our dwelling place
>   in all generations.
> Before the mountains were brought forth,
>   or ever you had formed the earth and the world,
>   from everlasting to everlasting you are God.
> You turn human beings back to dust,
>   and say, "Turn back, you mortals."[3]
> For a thousand years in your sight
>   are like yesterday when it is past,
>   or like a watch in the night. (90:1–4)

The words of these verses are a fitting reply to the questions posed by the psalmist in Psalm 89:

> How long, O LORD? Will you hide yourself forever?
>   How long will your wrath burn like fire?...
> LORD, where is your steadfast love of old,
>   which by your faithfulness you swore to David? (89:46, 49)

The singer of Psalm 90 reminds the Israelites that God has existed since before the mountains were brought forth and that God will be God "from everlasting to everlasting."

> How long, O LORD? Will you hide yourself forever? (89:46)

> A thousand years in your sight are like yesterday. (90:4)

Psalm 89 laments the broken covenant with David:

> But now you have spurned and rejected him;
>   you are full of wrath against your anointed.
> You have renounced the covenant with your servant;
>   you have defiled his crown in the dust. (89:38–39)

Why? Why has God renounced the covenant? Psalm 90's psalmist replies:

> For we are consumed by your anger;
>   by your wrath we are overwhelmed.
> You have set our iniquities before you,
>   our secret sins in the light of your countenance. (90:7–8)

Kingship: the "Grand Experiment"

The "grand experiment" of kingship in Israel has failed. The Israelites had demanded a king (1 Sam. 8:4–5). God warned them of the consequences of having a king (1 Sam. 8:11–18). The people persisted in their request, and God relented (1 Sam. 8:19–22). The remainder of the Deuteronomistic history records the story. Kingship in Israel resulted in the very things about which God had warned the people, and more. The kings, even the ones of David's line, broke the covenant over and over again. Second Kings characterizes Ahaz, the late-eighth-century B.C.E. king of Judah:

> He did not do what was right in the sight of the LORD his God, as his ancestor David had done…He even made his son pass through fire, according to the abominable practices of the nations whom the LORD drove out before the people of Israel. He sacrificed and made offerings on the high places, on the hills, and under every green tree. (2 Kings 16:2–4)

The description became even worse for Manasseh, king of Judah during the seventh century B.C.E.:

> He rebuilt the high places that his father Hezekiah had destroyed; he erected altars for Baal, made a sacred

pole...worshiped all the host of heaven, and served them...He built altars for all the host of heaven in the two courts of the house of the LORD. He made his son pass through fire; he practiced soothsaying and augury, and dealt with mediums and wizards...The carved image of Asherah that he had made he set in the house of the LORD. (2 Kings 21:3–6)

As a result, God declared:

I am bringing upon Jerusalem and Judah such evil that the ears of everyone who hears of it will tingle...I will cast off the remnant of my heritage, and give them into the hand of their enemies; they shall become a prey and a spoil to all their enemies, because they have done what is evil in my sight and have provoked me to anger, since the day their ancestors came out of Egypt, even to this day. (2 Kings 21:12–15)

Psalm 90: Remembrance of a Time in the Past

The days of the Davidic kingdom were over; the kings and the people had not been faithful to God's covenant. But hope remained. The words of Psalm 90 are placed on the lips of Moses, "the man of God." Moses represents a different time in the life of ancient Israel, a time before Manasseh, before Ahaz, before Solomon and David, before Saul and Samuel, and before the judges and Joshua and the occupation of the land. Moses was chosen to lead the Israelites out of slavery in Egypt, bring them to an encounter with their God at Mount Sinai, and take them to the border of the land God had promised to give to the ancestors. In the land the people would establish themselves with a king, a palace, and a temple. As we saw in chapter 4, during the time of the wilderness wandering, the Israelites had to rely completely on God to provide for, sustain, and protect them. The people had no earthly king, only God and the prophet Moses as leaders. Psalm 90, "a prayer of Moses, the man of God," reminded the Israelites of that different time in their history.

But it also reminded the people that the time in the wilderness was fraught with conflict. Over and over again in the books of Exodus and Numbers, we read about the people's complaints and God's responses. In Exodus 15, for example, just after the Israelites crossed the Reed Sea in safety, the people found they were short of water:

When they came to Marah, they could not drink the water of Marah because it was bitter...And the people complained against Moses, saying, "What shall we drink?" (Ex. 15:23–24)

In response:

> He cried out to the LORD; and the LORD showed him a piece
> of wood; he threw it into the water, and the water became
> sweet. (Ex. 15:25)

On the next leg of the journey, the people complained to Moses:

> "If only we had died by the hand of the LORD in the land of
> Egypt, when we sat by the fleshpots and ate our fill of bread; for
> you have brought us out into this wilderness to kill this whole
> assembly with hunger." (Ex. 16:3)

God responded with manna and quail (Ex. 16:4–36).[4] A short time later,
the people found themselves lacking water once again:

> The people quarreled with Moses, and said, "Give us water to
> drink…Why did you bring us out of Egypt, to kill us and our
> children and livestock with thirst?" (Ex. 17:2–3)

Again, God provided water.

In Exodus 32, we read that the Israelites had arrived at Sinai, the
mountain of the Lord. Moses had ascended into the smoke and fire of
the mountain to receive the Torah, the instructions of God for the
people. The Israelites waited in the camp below for Moses to return. But
they grew impatient:

> When the people saw that Moses delayed to come down from
> the mountain, the people gathered around Aaron, and said to
> him, "Come, make gods for us, who shall go before us; as for
> this Moses, the man who brought us up out of the land of
> Egypt, we do not know what has become of him." (Ex. 32:1)

So Aaron placed all of their gold pieces in a mold, cast it in a furnace,
and produced a "golden calf." The people declared:

> These are your gods, O Israel, who brought you up out of the
> land of Egypt. (Ex. 32:4)

God observed what was happening and commanded Moses:

> Go down at once! Your people whom you brought up out of
> the land of Egypt, have acted perversely; they have been quick
> to turn aside from the way that I commanded them…Now let
> me alone, so that my wrath may burn against them and I may
> consume them. (Ex. 32:7–10)

But Moses implored the LORD his God, and said, "O LORD, why does your wrath burn hot against your people, whom you brought out of the land of Egypt with great power and with a mighty hand?...Turn—שׁוּב *(šûb)*—from your fierce wrath; change your mind—נָחַם *(nāḥam)*—and do not bring disaster on your people." (Ex. 32:11–12)

In response:

The LORD changed his mind—נָחַם *(nāḥam)*—about the disaster that he planned to bring on his people. (Ex. 32:14)

In Exodus 32, Moses pleaded with God to turn—שׁוּב *(šûb)*—and change God's mind—נָחַם *(nāḥam)*—and God responded. In Psalm 90, a prayer of Moses, the man of God, we read:

Turn—שׁוּב *(šûb)*—O LORD. How long?
And change your mind—נָחַם *(nāḥam)*—concerning your
  servants. (90:13)

Only in Exodus 32 and Psalm 90 does a human being admonish God to turn—שׁוּב *(šûb)*—and change God's mind—נָחַם *(nāḥam)*. In both passages, that human being is Moses, pleading with God not to act against the Israelites in retribution for their sins. Moses dissuaded God from destroying the Israelites in the wilderness; perhaps Moses can dissuade God once again at the end of the Davidic monarchy. The Targum to Psalm 90, in fact, titles the psalm, "A prayer of Moses the prophet, when the people sinned in the desert."

Targum
Aramaic translations of and commentaries on the Hebrew Bible, completed during the early centuries of the common era

---

Not just Psalm 90 but the whole fourth book of the Psalter is dominated by the person of Moses. Outside of Book Four, Moses is mentioned only once in the Psalter (Ps. 77:21). In Book Four, he is referred to seven times (Pss. 90:1; 99:6; 103:7; 105:26; 106:16, 23, 32). David and the Davidic monarchy is not the focus of the book. Rather it is Moses and the time in the life of ancient Israel that Moses represents. Psalm 90 marks a turning point in the Psalter, a turn away from looking back to the days of King David and a turn toward looking forward to the reign of God as king over Israel once again, just as during the time of the wilderness wandering.

The Enthronement Psalms

Psalm 93 begins a series of enthronement psalms (93, 95–99). In chapter 2 we defined these as psalms that celebrate the enthronement of the Lord as king in the midst of the people of God.[5] These psalms may have been used in Jerusalem in pre-exilic times during the New Year celebration (Rosh Hashanah) just prior to the Feast of Tabernacles (Booths or *Sukkoth*), the fall harvest festival.[6] Sigmund Mowinckel maintains the following:

> The enthronement psalms salute Yahweh as the king, who has just ascended his royal throne to wield his royal power. The situation envisaged in the poet's imagination, is Yahweh's ascent to the throne and the acclamation of Yahweh as king; the psalm is meant as the song of praise which is to meet Yahweh on his 'epiphany', his appearance as the new, victorious king.[7]

We have no clear biblical evidence for such a festival, although some have cited the description of David bringing the ark of the covenant into Jerusalem in 2 Samuel as such a rite:

> David and all the house of Israel brought up the ark of the LORD with shouting, and with the sound of trumpet…They brought in the ark of the LORD, and set it in its place, inside the tent that David had pitched for it; and David offered burnt offerings and offerings of well-being before the LORD. When David had finished…he blessed the people in the name of the LORD of hosts, and distributed food among all the people. (2 Sam. 6:15–19)

Enuma Elish: the Enthronement of Marduk

In Babylon in the second millennium B.C.E., the god Marduk was enthroned at each New Year festival as king over the land and defeater of all the forces that challenged his rule. The epic story known as *Enuma Elish* was probably composed to support and justify Marduk's position as high god within the Babylonian pantheon. Evidence indicates that it was read on the fourth day of the Near Year festival.[8] The first portion of the epic is a history of the gods of Babylon:

> When on high (*Enuma Elish*) the heaven had not been named,
> firm ground below had not been called by name,
> there was nothing but primordial Apsu, their begetter,
> and Mummu-Tiamat, she who bore them all,
> their waters commingling as a single body;
> no reed hut had been matted, nor marsh land had appeared,
> when no gods whatever had been brought into being,
> uncalled by name, their destinies undetermined—
> then it was that the gods were formed within them.[9]

Soon the godly realm was well-populated, and the noise from the younger gods disturbed the elder gods, Tiamat and Apsu. They plotted to destroy the younger gods, but Apsu was prevented from doing so by the god Ea, who killed Apsu. Left on her own, Tiamat created an army of sea monsters to assist her in carrying out the task of destroying the noisy younger gods. Ea was not able to defeat Tiamat and her sea gods as he had Apsu, so the young gods appealed to Marduk, Ea's son, to take on the task.

Marduk agreed to go to battle against Tiamat on one condition. If he was successful, the young gods would acclaim him as king. The story continues in *Enuma Elish*:

> Forth came Marduk, the wisest of gods, your son,
> his heart having prompted him to set out to face Tiamat.
> He opened his mouth, saying unto me:
> If I indeed, as your avenger,
> am to vanquish Tiamat and save your lives,
> set up the assembly, proclaim supreme my destiny!
>
> When in Ubshukinna jointly you sit down rejoicing,
> let my word, instead of you, determine the fates.
> What I may bring into being shall be unalterable;
> neither shall the command of my lips be recalled nor changed!

The young gods agreed to Marduk's request:

> Joyfully they did homage: "Marduk is king!"
> They conferred on him scepter, throne, and vestment;
> They gave him matchless weapons that ward off the foes:
> "Go and cut off the life of Tiamat.
> May the winds bear her blood to places undisclosed."

Thus Marduk set out to destroy Tiamat and her sea monsters. He was, of course, successful. After the battle, he took the corpse of Tiamat and fashioned it into the heavens and the earth.

He split her like a shellfish into two parts:
half of her he set up and ceiled it as sky,
pulled down the bar and posted guards.
He bade them not allow her waters to escape.
He crossed the heavens and surveyed the regions…
He constructed stations for the great gods,
fixing their astral likenesses as the Images.
He determined the year by designating the zones:
he set up three constellations for each of the twelve months…
After he had appointed the days to the sun,
And had established the precincts of night and day,
He formed the clouds and filled them with water.
The raising of winds, the bringing of rain and cold,
Making the mist smoke, piling up Tiamat's poison:
These he appointed to himself, took into his own charge.
Putting her head into position he formed the mountains,
Opening the deep which was in flood,
He caused to flow from her eyes the Euphrates and Tigris,
Stopping her nostrils he left…,
He formed at her udder the lofty mountains,
Therein he drilled springs for the wells to carry off the water.
Thus he created heaven and earth…,
their bounds…established.

Humankind was created from the blood of a lesser god named
Kingu, who had acted as Tiamat's second-in-command in the battle
against the younger gods. Babylon was built as the city of Marduk, and
the gods celebrated the kingship of Marduk.

"His name shall be 'king of the gods of heaven and underworld'
    [LUGAL-DIMMER-ANKIA], trust in him!"
When they had given the sovereignty to Marduk,
They declared for him good fortune and success:
"Henceforth you will be the patron of our sanctuaries,
Whatever you command we will do."

Marduk is depicted in *Enuma Elish* as the one who conquers
Tiamat, the goddess of the sea, and her chaotic group of sea
monsters; as the one who forms and fashions the heavens and the
earth; as the one who reigns supreme over the gods and over the city
of Babylon; and as the final word of authority in matters pertaining
to Babylon.

The Enthronement of God

The enthronement psalms in Book Four of the Psalter depict Yahweh, the God of the Israelites, in much the same way. Using familiar language and poetic images, the psalmists convey the majesty of the God of the Israelites over all gods. God conquers the chaos of the sea, forms and fashions the heavens and the earth, reigns over the world from the temple in Jerusalem, and renders decisions in matter pertaining to the welfare of the people:

> The LORD is king, he is robed in majesty;
>> the LORD is robed, he is girded with strength.
> He has established the world; it shall never be moved...
> More majestic than the thunders of mighty waters,
>> more majestic than the waves of the sea,
>> majestic on high is the LORD! (93:1, 4)

> The LORD is a great God,
>> and a great King above all gods.
> In his hands are the depths of the earth;
>> the heights of the mountains are his also.
> The sea is his, for he made it,
>> and the dry land, which his hands have formed. (95:3–5)

> Zion hears and is glad,
>> and the towns of Judah rejoice,
>> because of your judgments, O God.
> For you, O LORD, are most high over all the earth;
>> you are exalted far above all gods. (97:8–9)

> Let the sea roar, and all that fills it;
>> the world and those who live in it.
> Let the floods clap their hands;
>> let the hills sing together for joy
> at the presence of the LORD, for he is coming
>> to judge the earth.
> He will judge the world with righteousness,
> and the peoples with equity. (98:7–9)

> The LORD is king; let the peoples tremble!
>> He sits enthroned upon the cherubim; let the earth quake!
> The LORD is great in Zion;
>> he is exalted over all the peoples. (99:1–2)

Indeed, Yahweh is king. The Israelites have no need of an earthly king.

Psalms 105 and 106

Book Four of the Psalter ends with two untitled psalms whose subject matter is the same, but whose forms are very different. Psalms 105 and 106 recount the history of the relationship between God and the ancient Israelites from the time of the ancestral stories in Genesis to the settlement in the land under the leadership of Joshua. But while Psalm 105 is a community hymn, Psalm 106 is a community lament.

Psalm 105 focuses on God and celebrates the goodness of God in providing for the Israelites throughout their history:

> He is mindful of his covenant forever...
> the covenant that he made with Abraham,
>   his sworn promise to Isaac...
> he allowed no one to oppress them;
>   he rebuked kings on their account...
> He sent his servant Moses,
>   and Aaron whom he had chosen...
> Then he brought Israel out with silver and gold,
>   and there was no one among their tribes who stumbled...
> He gave them the lands of the nations,
>   and they took possession of the wealth of the peoples. (105:8, 14, 26, 37, 44)

The story recounted in Psalm 106 is set in the same time and place in the life of ancient Israel. But Psalm 106 focuses on the Israelites' response to God's goodness and God's provision in spite of that response:

> Both we and our ancestors have sinned;
>   we have committed iniquity, have done wickedly.
> Our ancestors, when they were in Egypt,
>   did not consider your wonderful works;
> they did not remember the abundance of your steadfast love,
>   but rebelled against the Most High at the Sea of Reeds...
> They made a calf at Horeb
>   and worshiped a cast image.
> They exchanged the glory of God
>   for the image of an ox that eats grass...
> They did not destroy the peoples,
>   as the LORD commanded them,
> but they mingled with the nations
>   and learned to do as they did...

[But] for their sake God remembered the covenant,
    and showed compassion according to the abundance
    of his steadfast love. (106:6–7, 19–20, 34–35, 45)

The reader of Psalms 105 and 106 comes away from each with a very different "feeling." In Psalm 105, Israel celebrates its special relationship with the Lord, a relationship built on God acting in love and strength and the people responding in obedience and gratitude. Psalm 106 reminds the reader of Israel's true response to the Lord's many saving acts throughout its history. The same history; different views.

The pages of the Hebrew Bible contain many recitals of God's work in the history of the ancient Israelites. Joshua 24:1–13, Psalm 78, and Deuteronomy 6:20–24 are good examples:

> We were Pharaoh's slaves in Egypt, but the LORD brought us out of Egypt with a mighty hand. The LORD displayed before our eyes great and awesome signs and wonders against Egypt, against Pharaoh and all his household. He brought us out from there in order to bring us in, to give us the land that he promised on oath to our ancestors. (Deut. 6:21–23)

What sets Psalms 105 and 106 apart in this collection of "recitals" is the juxtaposition of two vastly divergent views of the same events.

In an essay entitled, *Abiding Astonishment: Psalms, Modernity, and the Making of History,* Walter Brueggemann discusses the importance of knowing one's history. History is the means by which a person or a group comes to an understanding of who they are, where they have come from, and where they are going. Reciting history makes one a participant in that history; the events live; the story creates a world; and the recitation helps to shape the future. Psalms 105 and 106 do just that for the reader of the Psalter. In these psalms, the "whole" story is told— God's gracious provision and Israel's obedience and rebellion. Brueggemann describes Psalm 105 as "a glad, unqualified celebration of God's gracious deeds," and Psalm 106 as "the same normative historical memory now turned to become a recital of Israel's sin, failure, and recalcitrance."[10] The world created by these psalms is a world of the reality of God's relationship with the Israelites. God provides; Israel obeys; Israel rebels; God is faithful.

Book Four of the Hebrew Psalter admonishes the Israelites to stop looking back and longing for the days of the Davidic dynasty, and to look ahead to the days of the reign of God as king over Israel, just as

God was king during the time of the wilderness wanderings. The community of faith which shaped the Psalter into its final form placed the untitled Psalms 105 and 106 side by side at the end of Book Four to remind the people of their history—all of it. And in so doing, the shapers of the Psalter provided a means by which that history—through its repeated recitation—could shape future communities of faith.

Psalm 106 ends with a plea to the Lord:

Save us, O LORD our God,
       and gather us from among the nations,
that we may give thanks to your holy name
       and glory in your praise. (Ps. 106:47)

And the Book ends with the usual doxology:

Blessed be the LORD, the God of Israel,
       from everlasting to everlasting.
And let all the people say, "Amen."
       Praise the LORD! (106:48)

At the end of Book Four, the Israelites in exile in Babylon have a rationale for survival in the new life circumstances in which they find themselves. Jerusalem and the temple are destroyed; the Davidic dynasty has failed. But God has not failed. If the Israelites remember and go back to the time of Moses and trust in God to be their king, then God will provide the stability and reason for being in a world that is no longer grounded in established modes of stability. Moses admonishes the people to go back and remember God's protection, provision, and sustenance. Book Five recounts how Yahweh as king will rule over the new Israel.

9

Book Five of the Psalter

Book Five of the Psalter begins with a recitation—in words of thanks (Ps. 107:1–3) and in story (107:4–32)—for God's delivering the Israelites from captivity and gathering them again to their own land. As we discussed in chapter 4 above, Cyrus, king of the Persians, allowed the Israelites to leave Babylon in 538 B.C.E. and return to Jerusalem. The people returned to their own land. They rebuilt the temple and resumed their religious practices. But they were vassals to the Persian Empire.[1] The Davidic dynasty had not been restored. The Israelites had to learn to rely on their God, Yahweh, as king.

In Book Five, King David reappears, after being absent in Books Three and Four. He leads the community of Israelites in celebrating God as king—as protector, provider, and sustainer—in this new life situation in which they find themselves. And at the heart of the book, in Psalm 119, the community discovers the way in which God will rule over them, the *Torah,* the instruction which God gave to the Israelites at Sinai. Acknowledge God as king and keep the *Torah,* and Israel will indeed survive as a viable entity in this new world.

Book Five of the Psalter consists of Psalms 107–150. The chart below indicates each psalm's superscription (if it has one)[2] and the psalm's *Gattung.*

Book Five	Superscription	Gattung
107	None	Community Hymn
108	A Song. A Psalm of David.	Community Lament
109	To the leader. Of David. A Psalm.	Individual Lament
110	Of David. A Psalm.	Royal

111	None	Individual Hymn of Thanksgiving
112	None	Wisdom
113	None	Community Hymn
114	None	Community Hymn
115	None	Community Hymn
116	None	Individual Hymn of Thanksgiving
117	None	Community Hymn
118	None	Individual Hymn of Thanksgiving
119	None	Wisdom
120	A Song of Ascents.	Individual Lament
121	A Song of Ascents.	Individual Hymn of Thanksgiving
122	A Song of Ascents. Of David.	Individual Hymn of Thanksgiving
123	A Song of Ascents.	Community Lament
124	A Song of Ascents. Of David.	Community Hymn
125	A Song of Ascents.	Community Hymn
126	A Song of Ascents.	Community Lament
127	A Song of Ascents. Of Solomon.	Wisdom
128	A Song of Ascents.	Wisdom
129	A Song of Ascents.	Community Hymn
130	A Song of Ascents.	Individual Lament
131	A Song of Ascents. Of David.	Individual Hymn of Thanksgiving
132	A Song of Ascents.	Royal
133	A Song of Ascents.	Wisdom
134	A Song of Ascents.	Community Hymn
135	None	Community Hymn
136	None	Community Hymn
137	None	Community Lament
138	Of David.	Individual Hymn of Thanksgiving
139	To the leader. Of David. A Psalm.	Individual Hymn of Thanksgiving
140	To the leader. A Psalm of David.	Individual Lament
141	A Psalm of David.	Individual Lament
142	A Maskil of David. When he was in the cave. A Prayer.	Individual Lament
143	A Psalm of David.	Individual Lament
144	Of David.	Royal

145	Praise. Of David.	Wisdom
146	None	Individual Hymn of Thanksgiving
147	None	Community Hymn
148	None	Creation
149	None	Community Hymn
150	None	Community Hymn

Psalm 107

Psalm 107, an untitled psalm, stands at the beginning of the Book. Its opening verses read:

> O give thanks to the LORD, for he is good;
>> for his steadfast love endures forever.
> Let the redeemed of the LORD say so,
>> those he redeemed from trouble
> and gathered in from the lands,
>> from the east and from the west,
>> from the north and from the south. (107:1–3)

The words seem to answer the appeal the psalmist made to God in the closing verse of Psalm 106:

> Save us, O LORD our God,
>> and gather us from among the nations,
> that we may give thanks to your holy name
>> and glory in your praise. (106:47)

Psalm 107 continues in verses 4–32 with the stories of four groups of people the Lord rescued from perilous circumstances: wanderers lost in the desert (vv. 4–9); prisoners (vv. 10–16); sick persons (vv. 17–22); and shipwrecked sailors (vv. 23–32). Each story follows a form:

• a description of the distress (vv. 4–5, 10–12, 17–18, and 23–27):
> Some were sick through their sinful ways,
>> and because of their iniquities endured affliction;
> they loathed any kind of food,
>> and they drew near to the gates of death. (vv. 17–18)

• a prayer to the Lord (vv. 6, 13, 19, and 28)
> Then they cried to the LORD in their trouble (v. 19)

- details of the deliverance (vv. 7, 14, 19–20, and 29)

> and he saved them from their distress;
> he sent out his word and healed them,
> and delivered them from destruction. (vv. 19–20)

- an expression of thanks (vv. 8–9, 15–16, 21–22, and 30–32)

> Let them thank the LORD for his steadfast love,
> for his wonderful works to humankind.
> And let them offer thanksgiving sacrifices,
> and tell of his deeds with songs of joy. (vv. 21–22)

In its original form, Psalm 107 most likely consisted only of verses 1–32 and was used at the temple in Jerusalem as a liturgy of thanksgiving for deliverance. Verses 33–42, which proclaim that the sovereign Lord can provide the people with all of their needs, appears to be a separate composition added to Psalm 107 at some point in its history. In its verses, we read that the Lord makes it possible for the hungry to dwell safely in the land and establish a city; to sow fields, plant vineyards, and gather a harvest; to have children and increase their cattle (vv. 36–38). The Lord pours contempt on rulers who oppress the people (vv. 39–40). The future of the upright is secured, and the unrighteous are left speechless (v. 42). The psalm closes with the words:

> Let [the one who is] wise—חָכָם (ḥākām)—give heed to these things,
> and consider the steadfast love of the LORD. (107:43)

Psalms of David

The next three psalms in Book Five, Psalms 108, 109, and 110, are "of David." In fact, fourteen of the forty-four psalms (32 percent) in Book Five are attributed to David. The reader will recall that in Book Three, only one psalm is "of David," and in Book Four, only two. In Book Five, David makes a dramatic reappearance in the story of the Psalter.

Psalm 108

Psalm 108 is a community lament which joins together portions of two psalms from Book Two of the Hebrew Psalter: Psalms 57:7–11 and 60:5–12. They are two of the thirteen psalms in the Hebrew Psalter that, in their superscriptions, recall specific historical events in the life of David. Psalm 57's superscription is:

> To the leader: Do Not Destroy. Of David. A Miktam, when he fled from Saul, in the cave.

Psalm 60's is:

> To the leader: according to the Lily of the Covenant. A Miktam
> of David; for instruction; when he struggled with Aram-
> naharaim and with Aram-zobah, and when Joab on his return
> killed twelve thousand Edomites in the Valley of Salt.

Psalm 108 is a poignant reminder to the reader of the very human
David so vividly portrayed in the Psalter and of the power of God to
defeat the enemy. The psalm closes with the following words:

> O grant us help against the foe,
>> for human—אָדָם (*'ādām*)—help is worthless.
> With God we shall do valiantly;
>> it is he who will tread down our foes. (vv. 12–13)

Erich Zenger summarizes the content of Psalm 108 as: "the salvation of
Israel as proof before all nations of the steadfast love—חֶסֶד (*ḥesed*)—
and the faithfulness—אֱמֶת (*ʾemet*)—of Yhwh and hence the revelation
of Yhwh's universal reign."[3]

Psalm 109 and 110

Psalm 109 is an individual lament of David, which petitions God to
punish the oppressors for their "wicked and deceitful mouths, words of
hate, and accusations" (vv. 2–4) and to vindicate the innocent psalmist.
It is followed by a royal psalm, giving the king assurance:

> The LORD is at your right hand;
>> he will shatter kings on the day of his wrath.
> He will execute judgment among the nations,
>> filling them with corpses;
> he will shatter heads
>> over the wide earth. (110:5–6)

Psalms 111 and 112

Following Psalm 110, the reader encounters two psalms, 111 and
112, composed in the acrostic style described in chapter 1. Each of the
very brief lines of the psalms begins with a successive letter of the
Hebrew alphabet.

112:1 הַלְלוּ יָהּ ׀

(א) אַשְׁרֵי־אִישׁ יָרֵא אֶת־יְהוָה

(ב)   בְּמִצְוֹתָיו חָפֵץ מְאֹד:

2   (ג)   גִּבּוֹר בָּאָרֶץ יִהְיֶה זַרְעוֹ

(ד)   דּוֹר יְשָׁרִים יְבֹרָךְ:

3   (ה)   הוֹן־וָעֹשֶׁר בְּבֵיתוֹ

(ו)   וְצִדְקָתוֹ עֹמֶדֶת לָעַד:

Psalms 113–118

Psalms 113–118 are known as the Egyptian Hallel psalms. In the Hebrew Psalter, none of the psalms in this collection has a superscription, but in the Septuagint, each is titled "Hallelujah"— "Praise the LORD"—a reflection and echo of the beginnings and/or endings of most of them. The psalms are all hymns (no laments occur in the group) and they are traditionally read during Passover, the Spring festival which commemorates and celebrates the Israelites' exodus from Egypt. Psalms 113 and 114 are read at the beginning of the celebration:

> Praise the LORD!
> Praise, O servants of the LORD;
>> praise the name of the LORD.
> Blessed be the name of the LORD
>> from this time on and forevermore. (113:1–2)

> When Israel went out from Egypt,
>> the house of Jacob from a people of strange language,
> Judah became God's sanctuary,
>> Israel his dominion...
> Tremble, O earth, at the presence of the LORD,
>> at the presence of the God of Jacob,
> who turns the rock into a pool of water,
>> the flint into a spring of water. (114:1–2, 7–8)

Psalms 115–118 are read at the conclusion of the celebration:

> The LORD has been mindful of us; he will bless us;
>> he will bless the house of Israel;
>> he will bless the house of Aaron;
> he will bless those who fear the LORD,
>> both small and great. (115:12–13)

Praise the LORD, all you nations!
  Extol him, all you peoples!
For great is his steadfast love toward us,
  and the faithfulness of the LORD endures forever.
Praise the LORD! (117:1–2)

With the LORD on my side I do not fear.
  What can mortals do to me?
The LORD is on my side to help me;
  I shall look in triumph on those who hate me.
It is better to take refuge in the LORD
  than to put confidence in mortals.
It is better to take refuge in the LORD
  than to put confidence in princes. (118:6–9)

Psalm 119: a Wisdom Acrostic

Following the Egyptian Hallel psalms is Psalm 119, a massive wisdom acrostic. Eight lines of the psalmic poem are given to each letter of the Hebrew alphabet, yielding a 176–line text. The psalm celebrates the goodness of the Torah and of the one who observes Torah Piety. It begins with the words:

Happy—אַשְׁרֵי *('ašrê)*—are those whose way is blameless,

who walk in the law—תּוֹרָה *(tôrāh)*—of the LORD. (119:1)

In Psalm 119 seven Hebrew words are used in synonymous interchange with the word "Torah" (which itself is used 25 times in the psalm):

עֵדָה *('ēdāh)*, translated as "decree" (used 23 times)

מִשְׁפָּט *(mišpāṭ)*, translated as "ordinance" (used 23 times)

חֹק *(ḥōq)*, translated as "statute" (used 22 times)

דָּבָר *(dābār)*, translated as "word" (used 22 times)

מִצְוָה *(miṣwāh)*, translated as "commandment" (used 22 times)

פִּקּוּד *(piqqûd)*, translated as "precept" (used 21 times)

אִמְרָה *('imrāh)*, translated as "promise" (used 19 times)

Psalm 119 is read at the Feast of Pentecost, the Spring festival fifty days after Passover. The Feast celebrates the giving of the Torah to Moses at Sinai during the wilderness wanderings. In the Hebrew Psalter, Psalm 119 has no superscription, but, like the Egyptian Hallel psalms which precede it, the Septuagint reads "Hallelujah."

Psalms 120–134: the Songs of Ascents

The superscriptions of Psalms 120–134 identify them as "Songs of Ascents," perhaps because of the frequent references to Jerusalem and Zion. The Songs of Ascents are the psalms traditionally read at the Feast of Tabernacles (or Booths, or *Sukkoth*) in the Autumn. The Feast of Tabernacles commemorates God's care for the Israelites during the time of the Wilderness Wanderings, reinforcing the "pilgrimage" theme of the Songs of Ascents.

An interesting aspect of The Songs of Ascents is the wide variety of psalm types included in this relatively small collection—individual and community laments (Pss. 120, 123, 126, 130), individual and community hymns (Pss. 121, 122, 124, 125, 129, 131, 134, 135, 136), wisdom psalms (Pss. 127, 128, 133), and a royal psalm (Ps. 132). The variety of *Gattungen* represented in the Songs of Ascents troubles many scholars. They question whether such an eclectic mix could ever have been a collection actually used in the life of ancient Israel. Michael Goulder has a reminder for us, however:

> Why should we think that a collection of psalms is not a unity because it contains pieces from different *Gattungen*? Have such critics never attended a church service that began with a confession, included lessons of instruction, hymns of praise and prayers, and ended perhaps with the General Thanksgiving?[4]

Psalm 133: a Study in Psalm Composition

One of the Songs of Ascents, Psalm 133—a Wisdom psalm—provides the reader with an interesting study in psalm composition. In its form in the Hebrew Psalter, the brief psalm reads thus:

> Behold, how very good and pleasant it is
>   when kindred live together in unity!
> It is like the precious oil on the head,
>   running down upon the beard,
> on the beard of Aaron,
>   running down over the collar of his robes.
> It is like the dew of Hermon,
>   which falls on the mountains of Zion.
> From there the LORD ordained his blessing,
>   life forevermore. (133:1–3)

In its position in the book of Psalms, Psalm 133 appears to be a proclamation of delight, sung by pilgrims traveling up to Jerusalem to celebrate the Feast of Tabernacles. It paints a picture of the sincere and simple pleasure of people who are bound together by their covenant with the Lord and who, having come from a great distance, anticipate with joy standing together in the courts of the temple and in sitting down together at the feast table. The celebrations of festivals at the Temple in Jerusalem transformed pilgrims coming from different places into a family that for a holy time ate and dwelt together. Psalm 133 was a song of greeting, of anticipation, and of celebration of that holy time.

But where did Psalm 133 come from? Was it composed especially for use as a Song of Ascents? Or is it, like many, or most, of the psalms in the Hebrew Bible, a traditional song of the community of ancient Israel which at some point was woven into the final form of, first the Songs of Ascents, and then the Hebrew Psalter?

The core of Psalm 133 may have been a wisdom or proverbial saying used in ancient Israel's social life—as a greeting when a person entered a home where people lived together in an extended family. The proverbial saying would have been the following:

> Behold, how very good and pleasant it is
> when kindred live together in unity!
> It is like the precious oil on the head,
> running down upon the beard,
> It is like the dew of Hermon.

Two metaphors are used to depict kindred dwelling together in unity—good oil and dew. Oil from the olive is and was an important commodity in the dry environment of the Near East. Olive oil is mixed with sweet-smelling spices and is used for hair and skin care. The oil is poured over the head, and, for men, runs down into the beard. A basic act of hospitality when visitors entered the home was to wash their feet and to pour soothing and refreshing oil on their heads. Mt. Hermon, located some 125 miles north of Jerusalem, is known for its abundant dew. In Palestine, which sees little rainfall between the months of April and October, dew is also an important commodity. Without the nightly accumulation of dew, the land would be parched and dry for many months of the year. So, like the olive oil poured as refreshment upon the visitors' heads, the nightly dew soothes and refreshes the land.

When we examine Psalm 133 in its "proverbial saying" form, we notice that all "religious" or "worship" references are gone. It is just a simple blessing with two visual, concrete images of that blessing—the oil and the dew. But with that simple saying, the visitor infused an ordinary event of life—entering someone else's home—with a sacred aspect. By speaking these words of greeting upon entering another's household, the visitor bade God to bless the household.

The ancient Israelite hearer of the Song of Ascents we call Psalm 133 would most likely have remembered the proverbial saying on which the psalm is based. But that saying, that blessing, was given special meaning by its religious additions. The oil poured upon the head in verse 2 is poured upon Aaron's head and runs down into his beard and onto the collar of his garments. Oil was used to anoint Aaron high priest of the ancient Israelites (Lev. 8:12). The psalm now celebrates the continued abundance of the anointing oil. The cup of ancient Israel runs over!

Mt. Hermon's abundant dew in verse 3 comes down upon Mt. Zion, and Jerusalem, the center of worship for ancient Israel, is soothed and refreshed. As the pilgrims approached the temple together as kindred, the unity—the oil and the dew—flowed down and was good and pleasant.

By singing Psalm 133 as one of the Songs of Ascents, the pilgrims going up to Jerusalem still celebrated the joy and goodness of dwelling together as brothers and sisters—they remembered the proverbial saying that was the foundation of Psalm 133. But the words of the whole psalm reminded the people that their family relationship was established not by blood, but by their mutual share in the covenant community of God. The Songs of Ascents prepared the pilgrims to celebrate together, as a family, as kindred living in oneness, the festivals of the Lord their God.

Thus Psalms 113–118, the "Egyptian Hallel Psalms," celebrate the Passover and deliverance from Egypt; Psalm 119, a wisdom psalm about Torah piety, commemorates the giving of the Torah at Mt. Sinai; and Psalms 120–134, the Songs of Ascents, celebrate the provisions of God during the wilderness wanderings. These twenty-two psalms, then, form a "collection of collections" of psalms read at particular celebrations in the life of ancient Israel.

Psalm 135–137

Psalms 135–137, all untitled psalms, each contribute in their own way to the story of Book Five of the Psalter. Psalm 135 is a community hymn which opens and closes with the "Hallelujah" that is typical of psalms in Book Five. The verb הָלַל (hālal) occurs eighty times in the Psalter, fifty-six times in Book Five.

Praise the LORD—הַלְלוּ יָהּ (hal^elû yāh)!
     Praise the name of the LORD;

give praise, O servants of the LORD...
Blessed be the LORD from Zion,
> he who resides in Jerusalem.
Praise the LORD—הַלְלוּ יָהּ *(hal'lû yāh)!* (135:1, 21)

Psalm 136 begins and ends with the words "O give thanks to the LORD, for he is good" (vv. 1,26). It narrates the great deeds of the Lord throughout Israel's history—creation (vv. 5–9); the deliverance from Egypt (vv. 10–12); the parting of the Red Sea (or Sea of Reeds) (vv. 13–15); the wilderness wanderings (v. 16); the giving of the land (vv. 17–22); and the continued protection of Israel (vv. 23–25)—using a fixed liturgical formula. Each verse ends with the refrain "for his steadfast love—חֶסֶד *(ḥesed)*—endures forever."

O give thanks to the Lord of lords,
> *for his steadfast love endures forever...*
who by understanding made the heavens,
> *for his steadfast love endures forever;*
who spread out the earth on the waters,
> *for his steadfast love endures forever...*
who divided the Sea of Reeds in two,
> *for his steadfast love endures forever;*
and made Israel pass through in the midst of it,
> *for his steadfast love endures forever...*
It is he who remembered us in our low estate,
> *for his steadfast love endures forever;*
and rescued us from our foes,
> *for his steadfast love endures forever...*
O give thanks to the God of heaven,
> *for his steadfast love endures forever.* (136:3, 5–6, 13–14, 23–26)

Psalm 137, a community lament, is perhaps the most difficult psalm to incorporate into the story of Book Five of the Psalter. The subject matter of this community lament is the exile in Babylon:

By the rivers of Babylon—
> there we sat down and there we wept
> when we remembered Zion.
On the willows there
> we hung up our harps.
For there our captors
> asked us for songs,
and our tormentors asked for mirth, saying,

> "Sing us one of the songs of Zion!"
> How could we sing the LORD's song
> in a foreign land? (137:1–4)

The disturbing words in verse 9, "Happy—אַשְׁרֵי (ʾašrê)—shall they be who take your little ones and dash them against the rock!" are difficult to maneuver. How may we understand them? J. Clinton McCann offers a helpful insight. He writes:

> In the face of monstrous evil, the worse possible response is to feel *nothing*. What *must* be felt is grief, rage, outrage. In their absence, evil becomes an acceptable commonplace. To forget is to submit to evil, to wither and die; to remember is to resist, be faithful, and live again…the psalmist in Psalm 137 submits his anger to God (notice that v. 7…is specifically addressed to God)…this submission of anger to God obviates the need for actual revenge on the enemy.[5]

For the postexilic community in Jerusalem, remembering the past—the distant past along with the immediate past—was important. The whole story informed the actions and ideas of this people struggling to maintain their identity in a new world.

Beginning with Psalm 138, Book Five returns to psalms "of David" in a group which runs through Psalm 145. The strong presence of David is emphasized by the fact that Psalms 138–143 are all psalms of an individual. Psalms 138 and 139 are individual hymns; Psalms 140–143 are individual laments.

Psalm 144

Psalm 144 is the third royal psalm in Book Five. It is categorized as royal because the central figure of the psalm is the king; but this psalm is an interesting composition. In verses 1–11, we hear echoes of a number of other psalms in the Hebrew Psalter:

- Psalm 8, in 144:3:

  O LORD, what are human beings—אָדָם (ʾādām)—that you regard them,
  or mortals—בֶּן אֱנוֹשׁ (ben ᵉnôš)—that you think of them?

- Psalm 39 in 144:4:

  [Human beings] —אָדָם (ʾādām)—are like a breath;
  their days are like a passing shadow.

• Psalm 18, another royal psalm, one with an historical superscription—
"a Psalm of David the servant of the LORD, who addressed the words
of this song to the LORD on the day when the LORD delivered him
from the hand of all his enemies, and from the hand of Saul"—
provides the inspiration for many of the phrases we encounter in the
first eleven verses of Psalm 144:

> Blessed be my rock (18:46=144:1)
> My fortress and my deliverer (18:2=144:2)
> He bowed the heavens also and came down (18:9=144:5)
> the hands of aliens (18:44, 45 = 144:7, 11)

James L. Mays writes about Psalm 144:

> The composer of Psalm 144 must have found in [Psalm 18] a
> promise for the psalmist's own time. So the psalmist composed
> a psalm of praise and prayer to the God who [according to verse
> 10 of Ps 144] "gives salvation to kings and rescues his servant
> David" as a context for petitions for deliverance from the aliens
> of the psalmist's time. By re-praying Psalm 18 in a new version,
> the writer appealed to the LORD to do for the people what the
> LORD has done for the LORD's servant David.[6]

In verse 12, the voice of Psalm 144 changes from first-person singular
language to first-period plural. It emphasizes the blessings that come
upon the people whose God is the Lord. In the last verse of the psalm,
we read the now-familiar wisdom words:

> Happy—אַשְׁרֵי (ʾašrê)—are the people to whom such blessings fall;
> Happy—אַשְׁרֵי (ʾašrê)—are the people whose God is the LORD.
> (144:15)

Psalm 145

In Psalm 145, "a praise of David," the reader encounters a masterful
wisdom composition in which David leads the people in acclaiming
God as king and in speaking the Lord's praises. David begins with his
personal remembrance and praise of the Lord:

> I will extol you, my God and King,
>   and bless your name forever and ever.
> Every day I will bless you,
>   and praise your name forever and ever. (145:1–2)

In verses 4–7, David's remembrance is mingled with the remembrance and praise of the generations of Israelites:

> One generation shall laud your works to another,
>> and shall declare your mighty acts.
> They shall celebrate the fame of your abundant goodness,
>> and shall sing aloud of your righteousness. (145:4, 7)

In verses 10–12, the praise of generations of Israelites is blended with the praise of remembrance of "all God's creation."

> All your works shall give thanks to you, O LORD,
>> and all your faithful shall bless you. (145:10)

The psalm ends with words that universalize the kingship of the Lord:

> My mouth will speak the praise of the LORD,
>> and all flesh will bless his holy name forever and ever.
> (145:21)

Thus the reader observes a movement in Psalm 145's praise from David alone to "the generations of Israelites" to all of creation. The personal praise of the individual psalmist becomes universal.

David ———→ The Generations ———→ All of Creation
of Israelites

The centerpiece of Psalm 145 is its acrostic structure. The psalm begins, in its *aleph* (א) line, with the words, "I will extol you, My God and King"—מֶלֶךְ (*melek*). And in the *kaf* (כ), *lamed* (ל), *mem* (מ) lines (the inverted letters of the word "king"—מֶלֶךְ [*melek*]), we read:

> (כ) They shall speak of the glory of your kingdom—מַלְכוּתְךָ
>> (*malkûtᵉkā*),
>> and tell of your power,
> (ל) to make known to all people[7] your mighty deeds,
>> And the glorious splendor of his kingdom—מַלְכוּתוֹ
>> (*malkûtô*).[8]
> (מ) Your kingdom—מַלְכוּתְךָ (*malkûtᵉka*) —is a kingdom—
>> מַלְכוּת (*malkût*)—for all times,
>> And your dominion (from the root מָשַׁל [*māšal*], a synonym
>> of מָלַךְ [*mālak*]) will be from generation to generation.
>> (145:11–13)

The repetition of the words from the root מָלַךְ *(mālak)* in these acrostic lines is striking. When we tie this phenomenon to the theme and content of Psalm 145, it seems we have the work of a wisdom writer cleverly emphasizing David's acknowledgement of the kingship of the Lord. And if David can acknowledge God as king, then all Israel and even all creation must join in.

Additional evidence for the importance of Psalm 145 in Jewish life comes from two sources. At Qumran, a form of Psalm 145 has each of the alphabetic lines of the psalm followed by the refrain, "Blessed is the LORD and blessed is his name forever and ever." So the psalm might have been read in a recitative manner, such as:

> (א) I will extol you my God and King,
> > and bless your name forever and ever.
> > > *Blessed is the Lord and blessed is his name forever and ever.*
> (ב) Every day I will bless you,
> > and praise your name forever and ever.
> > > *Blessed is the Lord and blessed is his name forever and ever.*
> (ג) Great is the Lord, and greatly to be praised;
> > his greatness is unsearchable.
> > > *Blessed is the Lord and blessed is his name forever and ever.*
> (145:1–3)

Psalm 145 is still one of the most popular psalms in synagogue liturgy and appears in the Jewish Prayer Book more than any of the other 149 psalms. The Jewish Babylonian Talmud states that Psalm 145 is to be recited three times a day and everyone who does so "may be sure that he is a child of the world to come" (*Berakot* 4b).

Psalms 146–150: Words of Doxology

In Psalms 146–150 the hearer is returned to the "Hallelujah" psalms, the type encountered earlier in Book Five. An Individual Hymn in Psalm 146 is followed in 147 by a Community Hymn and in 148 by a Creation psalm. Psalms 149 and 150 are Community Hymns.

- Psalm 146—Individual Hymn
  - Psalm 147—Community Hymn
    - Psalm 148—Creation Hymn
      - Psalms 149–150—Community Hallelujahs

As in Psalm 145, the praise rendered to the Lord in these closing Hallelujah psalms begins with the individual (read David?), extends to the community of Israel and finally takes in all of creation.

**David ——————▶ The Generations ——————▶ All of Creation
of Israelites**

Psalms 149 and 150 are the climax of the Psalter's final five psalms, psalms Walter Brueggemann describes as "glad abandonment"—a letting loose of self to voice confidence in a new reality that only God can bring about.[9]

> Praise the LORD!
> Sing to the LORD a new song,
>   his praise in the assembly of the faithful...
> Let the faithful exult in glory;
>   let them sing for joy on their couches. (149:1, 5)

> Praise the LORD...
> Praise him with trumpet sound;
>   praise him with lute and harp!
> Praise him with tambourine and dance;
>   praise him with strings and pipe...
> Let everything that breathes praise the LORD!
>   Praise the LORD! (150:1, 3–4, 6)

Book Five of the Psalter has no "doxology," in the sense that the other books of the Psalter do. The last five psalms in the Book (146–150) are read as the doxology of Book Five and of the whole Psalter.

Conclusions

Book Five leads the reader/hearer from the despair of exile in Babylon to the celebration of a new life in the land of Israel with God as king and the *Torah* as the guide for life. But the celebration was possible only at the *end* of the story of the Psalter. The postexilic community had to understand where it came from—the failed Davidic kingship—and where it was going—an identifiable entity within the vast Persian empire—before it could participate in the praise of a new life with Yahweh, its God, as king. Thus the Psalter was a story of survival in the changed and changing world with which the postexilic Israelite community was confronted.

What final words may we offer about the Psalter? How may we summarize its story and understand its transmission and survival within the postexilic Israelite community? That is the journey upon which we will embark in the next chapter.

10

How Then Shall We Read the Psalter?

The Hebrew Psalter is a masterful collection of songs from the life of ancient Israel. In its pages readers encounter heartfelt laments, hymns of awe at the creator God, praises to God for deliverance and healing, liturgies of thanksgiving, instructions in wise living, and celebrations of the kingship of the Lord over Israel and the whole earth. The Psalter is indeed a collection, often called the hymnbook of second-temple Judaism.

How did the postexilic community perceive and use the book of Psalms? The Psalter's external shape was that of a story of identity and existence for the postexilic community, but its internal form was that of traditional cultic material. Individuals, groups, priests, and Levites sang the psalms during various worship experiences at the sanctuaries and the temple. The words of the psalms were powerful. While their use in worship remained an important function of the psalms, the Psalter as a whole was read publicly to remind the Israelites of their story—the majestic reign of king David, the dark days of oppression and exile, the restoration of the glorious reign of Yahweh, and the surety that Israel could continue to exist as a "nation" in the ancient Near East.

Both uses of the psalms were important to the ongoing life of the postexilic community and worked together in a reciprocal relationship. Their liturgical (or worship) use influenced the meaning and significance of the psalms in their canonical (or story) context, and their canonical use influenced the meaning and significance of the psalms in their worship context.

Therefore, the Psalter is not a haphazard collection. The arrangement of the 150 psalms within their five books bears the marks of purposeful shaping.

Book One

The Psalter opens with words of wisdom concerning Torah Piety:

Happy are those...
(Whose) delight is in the law (*Torah*) of the LORD,
    and on his law (*Torah*) they meditate day and night. (1:1, 2)

It continues with a word of warning to the nations and their rulers to recognize the Lord as king over all:

Now therefore, O kings, be wise;
    be warned, O rulers of the earth.
Serve the LORD with fear,
    with trembling kiss his feet. (2:10–11)

Readers enter the Psalter with two admonitions: observe the Torah; give homage to the Lord as king.

Book One continues with thirty-nine psalms "of David." These thirty-nine psalms allow readers glimpses into every facet of David's life—the king, the human being, the warrior, the father, the seeker after God. The majority of the psalms in Book One are laments, which call God to act on behalf of the psalmist against enemies and oppressors.

The lament psalm is an appropriate *Gattung* for David and for David's time. The golden age of King David was fraught with strife and conflict between the Israelites and various foreign groups (especially the Philistines), among the Israelites themselves, and between various members of David's household. The court history recorded in Samuel and Kings is filled with the stories.

Now the Philistines gathered all their forces at Aphek, while the Israelites were encamped by the fountain that is in Jezreel. (1 Sam. 29:1)

Now the Philistines fought against Israel; and the men of Israel fled before the Philistines, and many fell on Mount Gilboa. (1 Sam. 31:1)

Once again the Philistines came up, and were spread out in the valley of Rephaim. (2 Sam. 5:22)

......

Saul sent messengers to David's house to keep watch over him, planning to kill him in the morning. (1 Sam. 19:11)

There was a long war between the house of Saul and the house of David. (2 Sam. 3:1)

Now a scoundrel named Sheba son of Bichri, a
    Benjaminite...sounded the trumpet and cried out,
        "We have no portion in David,
            no share in the son of Jesse!" (2 Sam. 20:1)

......

As the ark of the LORD came into the city of David, Michal daughter of Saul looked out of the window, and saw King David leaping and dancing before the Lord; and she despised him in her heart. (2 Sam. 5:16)

Absalom stole the hearts of the people of Israel...Absalom sent secret messengers throughout all the tribes of Israel, saying, "As soon as you hear the sound of the trumpet, then shout: Absalom has become king in Hebron!" (2 Sam. 15:6, 10)

Nathan said [to David], "My Lord the king, have you said, 'Adonijah shall succeed me as king, and he shall sit on my throne'? For today...[they] are now eating and drinking before him, and saying, 'Long live King Adonijah!'" (1 Kings 1:24–25)

David had much about which to complain to God:

I am the scorn of all my adversaries,
    a horror to my neighbors,
an object of dread to my acquaintances;
    those who see me in the street flee from me...
For I hear the whispering of many—
    terror all around!—
as they scheme together against me,
    as they plot to take my life. (Ps. 31:11, 13)

And David had much to ask of God:

Do not let me be put to shame, O LORD,
    for I call on you;
let the wicked be put to shame;
    let them go dumbfounded to Sheol.
Let the lying lips be stilled
    that speak insolently against the righteous
    with pride and contempt. (31:17–18)

Laments contain not only words of complaint and petition against those striving against the psalmist. Each lament also contains words of confidence (the Expression of Trust) that God can indeed accomplish what the psalmist requests, and each lament ends with the Expression of Praise and Adoration to the God of Israel.

> Blessed be the LORD
>> for he has wondrously shown his steadfast love to me
>> when I was beset as a city under siege.
> I had said in alarm,
>> "I am driven far from your sight."
> But you heard my supplications
>> when I cried out to you for help. (31:21–22)

> Love the LORD, all you his saints.
>> The LORD preserves the faithful,
>> but abundantly repays the one who acts haughtily.
> Be strong, and let your heart take courage,
>> all you who wait for the LORD. (31:23–24)

Words of trust, confidence, and praise are found at the end of each of David's psalms of lament in Book One.

The last psalm in Book One, Psalm 41, a hymn, is an extended form of the Expressions of Trust and Praise, placed on the lips of David.

> Happy are those who consider the poor;
>> the LORD delivers them in the day of trouble.
> The LORD protects them and keeps them alive;
>> they are called happy in the land.
>> You do not give them up to the will of their enemies.
> The LORD sustains them on their sickbed;
>> in their illness you heal all their infirmities. (41:1–3)

Psalm 41 begins with the wisdom word "happy"—אַשְׁרֵי ('ašrê), the same word with which Psalm 1 begins and Psalm 2 ends. When readers arrive at the end of Book One's story of David, the wisdom word "happy" sends them back to the beginning of the Psalter, back to words about Torah piety and about the Lord as king over all the peoples and nations. How may readers assert with the confidence of King David that the Lord is pleased with them, that the Lord will uphold them and will set them in the Lord's presence forever? Like David, they must observe Torah piety and acknowledge God as king over all.

Book Two

Book Two of the Psalter also contains many laments. But not all of them are placed on the lips of David. The Korahites, temple singers from the days of David and Solomon, mix their voices with David in singing the laments of Book Two. The Korahites, in fact, sing the first community lament of the Psalter:

> You have rejected us and abased us,
>> and have not gone out with our armies.
> You made us turn back from the foe,
>> and our enemies have gotten spoil.
> You have made us like sheep for slaughter,
>> and have scattered us among the nations. (44:9–11)

Fifteen psalms of David appear in the middle of Book Two (Pss. 51–65). Fourteen of them are laments. Eight are connected, in their superscriptions, with particular events in the life of David. These psalms remind readers once again that David's life was one of turmoil and strife; but they also depict a king who loved the Lord and strove to serve the Lord with great fervor. In Psalm 63, "when David was in the Wilderness of Judah," we read these words:

> O God, you are my God, I seek you,
>> my soul thirsts for you;
> my flesh faints for you,
>> as in a dry and weary land where there is no water.
> So I have looked upon you in the sanctuary,
>> beholding your power and glory.
> Because your steadfast love is better than life,
>> my lips will praise you.
> So I will bless you as long as I live;
>> I will lift up my hands and call on your name. (63:1–4)

The only untitled psalm in Book Two is Psalm 71, an individual lament, which may be read as the supplication of an aged person for God not to forget or forsake:

> O God, from my youth you have taught me,
>> and I still proclaim your wondrous deeds.
> So even to old age and gray hairs,
>> O God, do not forsake me,
> until I proclaim your might

> to all the generations to come...
> You who have made me see many troubles and calamities
>   will revive me again;
> from the depths of the earth
>   you will bring me up again. (71:17–18, 20)

Book Two ends with a psalm "of Solomon." A royal psalm, its words call on God to bestow upon the new king all of the attributes required to make the king successful in his reign:

> May he live while the sun endures,
>   and as long as the moon, throughout all generations.
> May he be like rain that falls on the mown grass,
>   like showers that water the earth.
> In his days may righteousness flourish
>   and peace abound, until the moon is no more.
> May the kings of Tarshish and of the isles
>   render him tribute,
> may the kings of Sheba and Seba
>   bring gifts.
> May all kings fall down before him,
>   all nations give him service. (72:5–7, 10–11)

The last verse of Psalm 72 reads:

> The prayers of David son of Jesse are ended. (72:20)

We may read Psalms 71 and 72 as the words of an aged David who turns the reigns of the kingdom over to his favored son Solomon. In the words of Psalm 71, David reminds God of David's faithfulness and asks God not to forget him in his old age. In Psalm 72, David seeks God's blessings upon Solomon, asking that he become a great king in the ancient Near East.

Book Three

After David died, Solomon reigned for forty years as king "in Jerusalem and over all Israel" (1 Kings 11:42). He oversaw the construction of the Temple in Jerusalem; he was renowned for his wisdom; he received gifts from many lands; he increased the wealth of Israel:

> Thus King Solomon excelled all the kings of the earth in riches
>   and in wisdom. The whole earth sought the presence of

Solomon to hear his wisdom, which God had put into his mind. Every one of them brought a present, objects of silver and gold, garments, weaponry, spices, horses, and mules, so much year by year. (1 Kings 10:23–25)

Solomon also married many foreign women. According to the Deuteronomistic history, he took seven hundred princesses as wives and had three hundred concubines. We read:

When Solomon was old, his wives turned his heart away after other gods; and his heart was not true to the LORD his God, as was the heart of his father David…Therefore the LORD said to Solomon, "Since this has been your mind and you have not kept my covenant and my statutes that I have commanded you, I will surely tear the kingdom from you and give it to your servant…I will not, however, tear away the entire kingdom; I will give one tribe to your son, for the sake of my servant David and for the sake of Jerusalem, which I have chosen." (1 Kings 11:4, 11, 13)

During the reign of Solomon's son, Rehoboam, the northern tribes rebelled against him and made Jeroboam king over them. From that time on Israel was a divided nation—Judah with Jerusalem as its capital in the south; Israel with Samaria as its capital in the north. Peace was not to be found in the land, internally or externally. Judah and Israel fought with one another; the nations surrounding the two pushed in upon them.

Book Three of the Psalter is made up of psalms sung by Asaph, the Korahites, and the Ezrahites, all temple singers during the reigns of David and Solomon. It opens with Psalm 73, a wisdom psalm. But its wisdom is very different from that of Psalm 1. Psalm 1 presents an ordered world where the righteous prosper and the wicked perish. The singer of Psalm 73 observes the opposite.

I was envious of the arrogant;
    I saw the prosperity of the wicked.
For they have no pain;
    their bodies are sound and sleek.
Pride is their necklace;
    violence covers them like a garment.
They scoff and speak with malice;
    loftily they threaten oppression.

> They set their mouths against heaven,
>> and their tongues range over the earth. (Ps. 73:3–4, 6, 8–9)

In despair, the psalmist enters the sanctuary of the Lord and there finds order in the seeming chaos of life.

> Indeed, those who are far from you will perish;
>> you put an end to those who are false to you.
> But for me it is good to be near God;
>> I have made the LORD God my refuge,
>> to tell of all your works. (73:27–28)

Community laments and community hymns dominate Book Three of the Psalter. David, the individual, gives way to the community of the faithful ones who are attempting to make sense of all that is going on around them.

> O God, why do you cast us off forever?
>> Why does your anger smoke against the sheep of your
>> pasture?
> Remember your congregation, which you acquired long ago,
>> which you redeemed to be the tribe of your heritage.
>> Remember Mount Zion, where you came to dwell. (74:1–2)

> Restore us again, O God of our salvation,
>> and put away your indignation toward us.
> Will you be angry with us forever?
>> Will you prolong your anger to all generations?
> Will you not revive us again,
>> so that your people may rejoice in you?
> Show us your steadfast love, O LORD,
>> and grant us your salvation. (85:4–7)

Near the end of Book Three, readers encounter Psalm 88, an individual lament of Heman the Ezrahite. A lament like no other in the Psalter, it is almost wholly composed of only one of the five elements of a lament, the Complaint. The invocation and petition are brief lines within the song, and the expression of trust and the expression of praise and adoration are missing completely. The psalm ends with the words:

> Your wrath has swept over me;
>> your dread assaults destroy me.
> They surround me like a flood all day long;

from all sides they close in on me.
You have caused friend and neighbor to shun me;
    my companions are in darkness. (88:16–18)

Psalm 88's lament is followed by a royal psalm, Psalm 89. As Psalm 88 is a lament like no other in the Psalter, Psalm 89 is a royal psalm like no other. It begins like other royal psalms, praising God for the kind provisions to the king of God's choosing.

I will sing of your steadfast love, O LORD, forever;
    with my mouth I will proclaim your faithfulness to all
    generations.
I declare that your steadfast love is established forever;
    your faithfulness is as firm as the heavens.
You said, "I have made a covenant with my chosen one,
    I have sworn to my servant David:
'I will establish your descendants forever,
    and build your throne for all generations.'" (89:1–4)

But the psalm takes a sudden turn in verse 38.

But now you have spurned and rejected him;
    you are full of wrath against your anointed.
You have renounced the covenant with your servant;
    you have defiled his crown in the dust.
You have removed the scepter from his hand,
    and hurled his throne to the ground.
You have cut short the days of his youth;
    you have covered him with shame.
Lord, where is your steadfast love of old,
    which by your faithfulness you swore to David? (89:38–39,
    44–45)

In 722, the Assyrians destroyed Samaria and annihilated the population of Israel. In 587, the Babylonians destroyed Jerusalem and took a major portion of Judah's population into captivity in Babylon. The nations of Israel and Judah had come to the end; Davidic kingship had come to an end; the people were in exile from their homeland. Were the people called Israel, the people called by God through Abraham and Sarah, through Moses and Aaron and Miriam, through Deborah and Gideon, through Samuel and David and Solomon, at an end?

Book Three of the Psalter ends with Israel lamenting and asking questions of their God. The kingdom of David, which stretched "from Dan to Beersheba" was no more. The people asked, "Who are we? Who will lead us? Who will help us to survive in our new world?"

Book Four

Book Four of the Psalter begins with "A Prayer of Moses, the man of God." It is the only psalm in the Hebrew Psalter so designated. In it, we find these words—placed on the lips of Moses:

> Turn, O LORD! How long?
> > Have compassion on your servants!
> Satisfy us in the morning with your steadfast love,
> > so that we may rejoice and be glad all our days.
> Make us glad as many days as you have afflicted us,
> > and as many years as we have seen evil.
> Let your work be manifest to your servants,
> > and your glorious power to their children.
> Let the favor of the LORD our God be upon us,
> > and prosper the work of our hands—
> > O prosper the work of our hands! (90:13–17)

Through Moses, the people of Israel admonish the Lord to turn and restore them and make them glad. The Israelites cannot go back to the days of King David. They can only go forward. And the only way forward is to remember the Lord who called Abraham and Sarah; who blessed Jacob and Leah and Rachel with a multitude of offspring; who led the people to Egypt and freed them from that place under the leadership of Moses and Miriam and Aaron; who gave the Israelites the land of Canaan; and who raised up judges to lead the Israelites against their foes. To remember the Lord who called, provided for, protected, and sustained the people throughout centuries of their existence. And believe that this God can again call and bless and lead and give.

Enthronement psalms, celebrating the enthronement of the Lord as king—rather than a king of the Davidic line, dominate Book Four of the Psalter.

> The LORD is king, he is robed in majesty;
> > the LORD is robed, he is girded with strength. (93:1)

> For the LORD is a great God,
> > and a great King above all gods. (95:3)

Say among the nations, "The LORD is king!
>   The world is firmly established; it shall never be moved.
>   He will judge the peoples with equity." (96:10)

Mighty King, lover of justice,
>   you have established equity;
you have executed justice
>   and righteousness in Jacob.
Extol the LORD our God;
>   worship at his footstool.
>   Holy is he! (99:4–5)

Could the people of God survive and continue to exist in this new situation? Yes, if they acknowledged that God and not a human of the line of David was to be their king. God would be their king, just as God had been their king during the time of the ancestors, the exodus, and the wilderness wanderings. At the end of Book Four, Psalm 105 reminds the people how God provided for, protected, and sustained them throughout their history.

He is the LORD our God;
>   his judgments are in all the earth.
He is mindful of his covenant forever,
>   of the word that he commanded, for a thousand generations,
the covenant that he made with Abraham,
>   his sworn promise to Isaac,
which he confirmed to Jacob as a statute,
>   to Israel as an everlasting covenant...
He sent his servant Moses,
>   and Aaron whom he had chosen.
They performed his signs among them,
>   and miracles in the land of Ham...
Then he brought Israel out with silver and gold,
>   and there was no one among their tribes who stumbled...
He gave them the lands of the nations,
>   and they took possession of the wealth of the peoples.
>   (105:7–10, 26–27, 37, 44)

But the psalm immediately following, Psalm 106, reminds the people of their unfaithfulness to the sustaining God.

Both we and our ancestors have sinned;
>   we have committed iniquity, have done wickedly...

> They were jealous of Moses in the camp,
>> and of Aaron, the holy one of the LORD…
> They made a calf at Horeb
>> and worshiped a cast image…
> They grumbled in their tents,
>> and did not obey the voice of the LORD…
> Many times he delivered them,
>> but they were rebellious in their purposes,
>> and were brought low through their iniquity.
> Nevertheless he regarded their distress
>> when he heard their cry.
> For their sake he remembered his covenant,
>> and showed compassion according to the abundance of his
>> steadfast love. (106:6, 16, 19, 25, 43–44)

In 539, the Persian army, under the leadership of Cyrus II, captured Babylon, the capital city of the Babylonian Empire. In 538, Cyrus issued a decree allowing captive peoples to return to their homelands, rebuild, and resume their religious practices. But the repatriated peoples would remain part of the vast Persian Empire, subject to Persian law. For the Israelites, it meant that their temple could be rebuilt, their religious practices could continue, but the nation-state under the leadership of a king of the line of David would not be restored.

God had been king over the Israelites; God could be king once again. But the message was: Remember the past, and don't make the same mistakes in the future. Trust in God as king; heed God's voice; celebrate God's goodness. Psalm 106 ends with the words:

> Save us, O LORD our God,
>> and gather us from among the nations,
> that we may give thanks to your holy name
>> and glory in your praise. (106:47)

Book Five

Book Five of the Psalter begins with Psalm 107, a community hymn celebrating God's graciousness in delivering people from perilous circumstances. It opens with the words:

> O give thanks to the LORD, for he is good;
>> for his steadfast love endures forever.
> Let the redeemed of the LORD say so,
>> those he redeemed from trouble

and gathered in from the lands,
>   from the east and from the west,
>   from the north and from the south. (107:1–3)

Beginning in verse 33, the psalm outlines numerous beneficial acts the sovereign God is able to do on behalf of the people. The people may dwell in safety, establish a town, plant a vineyard, reap a harvest, be blessed with children and cattle, be defended against the enemy, and have their future secured. How may the people have all of this? Psalm 107 ends with the words:

> Let the one who is wise—חָכָם *(ḥākām)*—give heed to these things, and consider the steadfast love of the LORD. (107:43)

Beginning with Psalm 108, David makes a dramatic reappearance in the Hebrew Psalter. Psalms 108–110; 122; 124; 131; 138–145 are "of David." David's voice returns, leading the Israelites in praise of God as king over them.

> With my mouth I will give great thanks to the LORD;
>   I will praise him in the midst of the throng.
> For he stands at the right hand of the needy,
>   to save them from those who would condemn them to death.
>   (109:30–31)

> I bow down toward your holy temple
>   and give thanks to your name for your steadfast love and your
>   faithfulness;
>   for you have exalted your name and your word
>   above everything.
> On the day I called, you answered me,
>   you increased my strength of soul. (138:2–3)

> I remember the days of old,
>   I think about all your deeds,
>   I meditate on the works of your hands.
> I stretch out my hands to you;
>   my soul thirsts for you like a parched land. (143:5–6)

In the middle of Book Five of the Psalter, with psalms of David surrounding them, are passages included at Jewish celebrations:

- Psalms 113–118, the Egyptian Hallel, recited in Judaism at Passover
- Psalm 119, a wisdom acrostic about Torah piety, recited in Judaism at the Feast of Pentecost

- Psalms 120–134, the Songs of Ascents, recited in Judaism at the Feast of Booths or Tabernacles.

David leads, and the people join in to celebrate the God who created, sustained, protected, and guided them throughout their history. The last psalm of David in Book Five is Psalm 145, a masterful acrostic structure that celebrates the kingship of God over Israel and all of creation. David begins the celebration in verses 1 and 2:

> I will extol you, my God and King.
>> and bless your name forever and ever. (145:1)

Israel joins in verse 4:
> One generation shall laud your works to another, and shall
>> declare your mighty acts. (145:4)

All creation is called upon to praise the Lord in verse 10:
> All your works shall give thanks to you, O LORD,
>> and all your faithful shall bless you. (145:10)

In verses 8–9, readers are reminded of God's words of self-description, spoken to Moses at Sinai:

> The LORD is gracious and merciful, slow to anger and abounding
>> in steadfast love
> The LORD is good to all,
>> and his compassion is over all that he has made. (145:8–9 =
>> Ex. 34:6–7)

David leads the praise of God as king; Israel and all creation join in.

> My mouth will speak the praise of the LORD, and all flesh will
>> bless his holy name forever and ever. (145:21)

The Hebrew Psalter ends with five doxological psalms which bring the songs of the Psalter to a climax of praise to God the king:

> The LORD reigns forever, your God, O Zion, for all generations.
>> Praise the LORD! (146:10)

> Kings of the earth and all peoples, princes and all rulers of the
>> earth!
> Young men and women alike, old and young together!
> Let them praise the name of the LORD, for his name alone is
>> exalted; his glory is above earth and heaven. (148:11–13)

Praise the LORD! Sing to the LORD a new song,
    his praise in the assembly of the faithful.
Let Israel be glad in its Maker;
    let the children of Zion rejoice in their King. (149:1–2)

Why did Israel survive? Because Israel found a way to shape its poetry and prose—its traditional literature—into a meaningful story of identity. And with that story, the Israelites were (and are) able to remain the people of God in the midst of the changing world of which they found (and find) themselves a part.

Conclusion

In the introduction to *The Intellectual Adventure of Ancient Man: An Essay on Speculative Thought in the Ancient Near East,* Henri and H. A. Frankfort discuss humankind's attempt to find "intellectually satisfying" answers to basic questions of existence, questions like: "How did our world come into being?" "Has life always been the way it is?" "Will it always remain the same?" The Frankforts call the process of arriving at answers to these questions "speculative thought." They observe: "We may say that speculative thought attempts to underpin the chaos of experience so that it may reveal the features of a structure—order, coherence, and meaning."[1] In ancient Mesopotamia, for example, the rainstorm that ended a drought was not explained as resulting from a change in atmospheric conditions. Rather, the giant bird god Anzu devoured the Bull of Heaven, whose hot breath had scorched the land. It then spread its wings over the sky to form the black rain clouds. Mesopotamian society fulfilled its need to structure the phenomenal world by personifying natural forces as gods. The intervention of Anzu was a satisfying explanation for the coming of rain to end a drought. In the same way, Israel survived because the postexilic community found a satisfying rationale for survival. King, court, and temple were gone, but Israel survived because it appropriated and shaped its traditional and cultic material into a constitutive document of identity, the Hebrew scriptures. And the Psalter was part of that constitutive document. With their God, Yahweh, as king, the nation of ancient Israel could continue to exist as an identifiable entity in the vast empires of which it was a part. The postexilic community indeed found a way to "underpin the chaos of experience [and] reveal the features of a structure—order, coherence, and meaning."[2] Yahweh was king, regardless of the external exigencies of life. That affirmation was central to the survival and future of the postexilic Israelite community, and it remains central to the survival and future of believing communities today. The Lord is king. Hallelujah! הַלְלוּ יָהּ

APPENDIX 1

Psalm Superscriptions and *Gattungen*

Book One	Superscription	Gattung
1	None	Wisdom
2	None	Royal
3	A Psalm of David, when he fled from his son Absalom.	Individual Lament
4	To the leader: with stringed instruments. A Psalm of David.	Individual Lament
5	To the leader: for the flutes. A Psalm of David.	Individual Lament
6	To the leader: with stringed instruments; according to the Sheminith. A Psalm of David.	Individual Lament
7	A Shiggaion of David, which he sang to the LORD concerning Cush, a Benjaminite.	Individual Lament
8	To the leader: according to the Gittith. A Psalm of David.	Creation
9	To the leader: according to Muthlabben. A Psalm of David.	Individual Lament
10	(A Psalm of David)	Individual Lament
11	To the leader. Of David.	Individual Lament
12	To the leader: according to the Sheminith. A Psalm of David.	Community Lament
13	To the leader. A Psalm of David.	Individual Lament
14	To the leader. Of David.	Community Lament
15	A Psalm of David.	Community Hymn
16	A Miktam of David.	Individual Lament
17	A Prayer of David.	Individual Lament
18	To the leader. A Psalm of David the servant of the LORD, who addressed the words of this song to the LORD on the day when the LORD delivered him from the hand of all his enemies, and from the hand of Saul. He said:	Royal
19	To the leader. A Psalm of David.	Creation

20	To the leader. A Psalm of David.	Royal
21	To the leader. A Psalm of David.	Royal
22	To the leader: according to The Deer of the Dawn. A Psalm of David.	Individual Lament
23	A Psalm of David.	Individual Hymn of Thanksgiving
24	Of David. A Psalm.	Community Hymn
25	Of David.	Individual Lament
26	Of David.	Individual Lament
27	Of David.	Individual Lament
28	Of David.	Individual Lament
29	A Psalm of David.	Community Hymn
30	A Psalm. A Song at the dedication of the temple. Of David.	Individual Hymn of Thanksgiving
31	To the leader. A Psalm of David.	Individual Lament
32	Of David. A Maskil.	Wisdom
33	(Of David)	Community Hymn
34	Of David, when he feigned madness before Abimelech, so that he drove him out, and he went away.	Individual Hymn of Thanksgiving
35	Of David.	Individual Lament
36	To the leader. Of David, the servant of the LORD.	Individual Lament
37	Of David.	Wisdom
38	A Psalm of David, for the memorial offering.	Individual Lament
39	To the leader: to Jeduthun. A Psalm of David.	Individual Lament
40	To the leader. Of David. A Psalm.	Individual Lament
41	To the leader. A Psalm of David.	Individual Hymn of Thanksgiving

Book Two	Superscription	Gattung
42	To the leader. A Maskil of the Korahites.	Individual Lament
43	(a Maskil of the Korahites)	Individual Lament
44	To the leader. Of the Korahites. A Maskil.	Community Lament
45	To the leader: according to Lilies. Of the Korahites. A love song.	Royal
46	To the leader. Of the Korahites. According to Alamoth. A Song.	Community Hymn

47	To the leader. Of the Korahites. A Psalm.	Enthronement
48	A Song. A Psalm of the Korahites.	Community Hymn
49	To the leader. Of the Korahites. A Psalm.	Wisdom
50	A Psalm of Asaph.	Community Hymn
51	To the leader. A Psalm of David, when the prophet Nathan came to him, after he had gone in to Bathsheba.	Individual Lament
52	To the leader. A Maskil of David, when Doeg the Edomite came to Saul and said to him, "David has come to the house of Ahimelech."	Individual Lament
53	To the leader: according to Mahalath. A Maskil of David.	Community Lament
54	To the leader: with stringed instruments. A Maskil of David, when the Ziphites went and told Saul, "David is in hiding among us."	Individual Lament
55	To the leader: with stringed instruments. A Maskil of David.	Individual Lament
56	To the leader: according to The Dove on Far-off Terebinths. Of David. A Miktam, when the Philistines seized him in Gath.	Individual Lament
57	To the leader: Do Not Destroy. Of David. A Miktam, when he fled from Saul, in the cave.	Individual Lament
58	To the leader: Do Not Destroy. Of David. A Miktam.	Community Lament
59	To the leader: Do Not Destroy. Of David. A Miktam, when Saul ordered his house to be watched in order to kill him.	Individual Lament
60	To the leader: according to the Lily of the Covenant. A Miktam of David; for instruction; when he struggled with Aram-naharaim and with Aram-zobah, and when Joab on his return killed twelve thousand Edomites in the Valley of Salt.	Community Lament
61	To the leader: with stringed instruments. Of David.	Individual Lament
62	To the leader: according to Jeduthun. A Psalm of David.	Individual Lament
63	A Psalm of David, when he was in the Wilderness of Judah.	Individual Lament
64	To the leader. A Psalm of David.	Individual Lament
65	To the leader. A Psalm of David. A Song.	Creation
66	To the leader. A Song. A Psalm.	Individual Hymn of Thanksgiving
67	To the leader: with stringed instruments. A Psalm. A Song.	Community Hymn
68	To the leader. Of David. A Psalm. A Song.	Community Hymn

69	To the leader: according to Lilies. Of David.	Individual Lament
70	To the leader, Of David, for the memorial offering.	Individual Lament
71	None	Individual Lament
72	Of Solomon.	Royal

Book Three	Superscription	Gattung
73	A Psalm of Asaph.	Wisdom
74	A Maskil of Asaph.	Community Lament
75	To the leader: Do Not Destroy. A Psalm of Asaph. A Song.	Community Hymn
76	To the leader: with stringed instruments. A Psalm of Asaph. A Song.	Community Hymn
77	To the leader: according to Jeduthun. Of Asaph. A Psalm.	Individual Lament
78	A Maskil of Asaph.	Wisdom
79	A Psalm of Asaph.	Community Lament
80	To the leader: on Lilies, a Covenant. Of Asaph. A Psalm.	Community Lament
81	To the leader: according to The Gittith. Of Asaph.	Community Hymn
82	A Psalm of Asaph.	Community Hymn
83	A Song. A Psalm of Asaph.	Community Lament
84	To the leader: according to the Gittith. Of the Korahites. A Psalm.	Individual Hymn of Thanskgiving
85	To the leader. Of the Korahites. A Psalm.	Community Lament
86	A Prayer of David.	Individual Lament
87	Of the Korahites. A Psalm. A Song.	Individual Hymn of Thanksgiving
88	A Song. A Psalm of the Korahites. To the leader: according to Mahalath Leannoth. A Maskil of Heman the Ezrahite.	Individual Lament
89	A Maskil of Ethan the Ezrahite.	Royal

Book Four	Superscription	Gattung
90	A Prayer of Moses, the man of God.	Community Lament
91	None	Individual Hymn of Thanksgiving
92	A Psalm. A Song for the Sabbath Day.	Individual Hymn of Thanksgiving
93	None	Enthronement
94	None	Individual Lament

95	None	Enthronement
96	None	Enthronement
97	None	Enthronement
98	A Psalm.	Enthronement
99	None	Enthronement
100	A Psalm of Thanksgiving.	Community Hymn
101	Of David. A Psalm.	Royal
102	A prayer of one afflicted, when faint and pleading before the Lord.	Individual Lament
103	Of David.	Individual Hymn of Thanksgiving
104	None	Creation
105	None	Community Hymn
106	None	Community Lament

Book Five	Superscription	Gattung
107	None	Community Hymn
108	A Song. A Psalm of David.	Community Lament
109	To the leader. Of David. A Psalm.	Individual Lament
110	Of David. A Psalm.	Royal
111	None	Individual Hymn of Thanksgiving
112	None	Wisdom
113	None	Community Hymn
114	None	Community Hymn
115	None	Community Hymn
116	None	Individual Hymn of Thanksgiving
117	None	Community Hymn
118	None	Individual Hymn of Thanksgiving
119	None	Wisdom
120	A Song of Ascents.	Individual Lament
121	A Song of Ascents.	Individual Hymn of Thanksgiving
122	A Song of Ascents. Of David.	Individual Hymn of Thanksgiving
123	A Song of Ascents.	Community Lament
124	A Song of Ascents. Of David.	Community Hymn
125	A Song of Ascents.	Community Hymn

126	A Song of Ascents.	Community Lament
127	A Song of Ascents. Of Solomon.	Wisdom
128	A Song of Ascents.	Wisdom
129	A Song of Ascents.	Community Hymn
130	A Song of Ascents.	Individual Lament
131	A Song of Ascents. Of David.	Individual Hymn of Thanksgiving
132	A Song of Ascents.	Royal
133	A Song of Ascents.	Wisdom
134	A Song of Ascents.	Community Hymn
135	None	Community Hymn
136	None	Community Hymn
137	None	Community Lament
138	Of David.	Individual Hymn of Thanksgiving
139	To the leader. Of David. A Psalm.	Individual Hymn of Thanksgiving
140	To the leader. A Psalm of David.	Individual Lament
141	A Psalm of David.	Individual Lament
142	A Maskil of David. When he was in the cave. A Prayer.	Individual Lament
143	A Psalm of David.	Individual Lament
144	Of David.	Royal
145	Praise. Of David.	Wisdom
146	None	Individual Hymn of Thanksgiving
147	None	Community Hymn
148	None	Creation
149	None	Community Hymn
150	None	Community Hymn

An Explanation of Technical Terms in Psalm Superscriptions

The superscriptions of the psalms in the Hebrew Psalter contain a number of words which are difficult to define and some which are simply untranslatable. We may divide these words into three major categories:

I. Titles That Describe Poetic Forms

1. Psalm: מִזְמוֹר *(mizmôr)*

Because fifty-seven psalms are described as *"mizmôr"* in their superscriptions, we call the poems in the Hebrew Psalter "psalms." The Hebrew root of the word is זָמַר *(zāmar)* and means "to sing and/or to play a musical instrument."

2. Song: שִׁיר *(šîr)*

Thirty psalms are described as *"šîr."* The meaning of the Hebrew root is almost synonymous with *"mizmôr"* except that *"šîr"* refers only to "singing" and not to the "playing of musical instruments." Sixteen psalms of the thirty psalms which are designated in their superscriptions as *"šîr"* have dual designations: *"šîr"* and *"mizmôr"*: Psalms 30, 48, 65–68, 75, 76, 83, 87, 88, 92, and 108.

3. Maskil: מַשְׂכִּיל *(maśkîl)*

Thirteen psalms (Pss. 32, 42, 44, 45, 52–55, 74, 78, 88, 89, and 142) are designated as *"maśkîl."* The Hebrew root of the word is שָׂכַל *(śākal)*, and in the verbal stem in which we find the word in the Psalter, it means "to have insight, to teach." Scholars believe that the *"maśkîl"* is meant to be an artistic or teaching song.

4. Miktam: מִכְתָּם *(miktām)*

Psalms 16 and 56–60 are called *"miktām"* in their superscriptions. A number of meanings have been suggested for this word. The Hebrew root is כָּתַם (kātam). It occurs in the Hebrew Bible in only one place outside the Psalter (in Jer. 2:22), and it means "to be inscribed, to be written," with the idea of "to be made permanent." Therefore, a plausible meaning for "miktām" is "a carved inscription," indicating perhaps that these prayers were written down and deposited at the temple so that they could be offered to God over and over again.

5. Prayer: תְּפִלָּה (t^epillāh)

Psalms 17, 86, 90, 120, and 142 are called "t^epillāh." The Hebrew root of the word is פָּלַל (pālal) which means, in the verbal stem in which we find it in the Hebrew Psalter, "to pray." The "t^epillāh" may be described as a prayer of lament, asking God to intercede on the psalmist's behalf.

6. Shiggaion: / שִׁגָּיוֹן (šiggāyôn)

Psalm 7 is described in its superscription as a "šiggāyôn." The Hebrew root of the word is probably שָׁגָה (šāgāh), and may be related to the Akkadian word for "lamentation."

7. Praise: תְּהִלָּה (t^ehillāh)

Psalm 145 is called a "t^ehillāh." The Hebrew root of the word is הָלַל (hālal), the same root for the word "hallelujah," found throughout the Hebrew Psalter.

II. Titles That Indicate Musical Designations or Liturgical Instructions

1. To the Leader: לַמְנַצֵּחַ (lamnaṣṣēaḥ)

Fifty-five psalms, mostly in Books One, Two, and Three (Pss. 1–89), include this designation in their superscriptions. The Hebrew root of the word is נָצַח (nāṣaḥ), which means "to superintend, to be chief." As we saw in chapter 3, the preposition לְ (l^e) on the front of the word may be translated as "to, for, at the direction of, of." Thus we may translate the word as "to the leader," "for the leader," "at the direction of the leader," or "of the leader"—with "leader" being understood as the choir director or the chief musician of the temple singers and musicians.

2. With Stringed Instruments: בִּנְגִינוֹת (binginôt)

Psalms 4, 6, 54, 55, 61, 67, and 76 are marked with this instruction in their superscriptions. The Hebrew root of the word is / נָגַן (nāgan), which means "to touch the strings." The psalms with this designation were probably sung to the accompaniment of stringed instruments.

3. To/According to Jeduthun /לִידוּתוּן / עַל־יְדוּתוּן (lîdûtûn / 'al yᵉdûtûn)

This superscription appears in two forms: "to Jeduthun" (in Ps. 39) and "according to Jeduthun" (in Pss. 62 and 72). "yᵉdûtûn" is the name of a family of keepers of the temple which appears in 1 Chronicles 9:16; 16:38, 41; 25:1, 3, 6; and in 2 Chronicles 5:12.

4. For the Memorial Offering לְהַזְכִּיר (lᵉhazkîr)

Psalms 38 and 70 contain this note in their superscriptions. The Hebrew root of the word is זָכַר (zākar), and in its form in these superscriptions, means "to cause to remember." These psalms were most likely recited during some ceremony of remembrance at the temple.

5. For the Flutes אֶל־הַנְּחִילוֹת ('el hannᵉhîlôt)

This designation occurs only in Psalm 5. The Hebrew root of the word is most likely חָלַל (hālal), which means "to be pierced, to be perforated," thus the translation "flute." In 1 Samuel 10:5, the חָלִיל (hālîl) is a musical instrument used by a group of prophets to achieve a state of ecstasy.

III. Directions concerning the Tune or Style of Music to Be Used

1. Do Not Destroy אַל־תַּשְׁחֵת ('al tašhet)

This direction occurs in Psalms 57, 58, 59, and 75. All we can really say about it is that apparently "'al tašhet" was a particular melody or recitative style that was well-known at the temple in Jerusalem.

2. According to the Gittith עַל־הַגִּתִּית ('al haggittît)

Psalms 8, 81, and 84 include this direction in their superscriptions. "Gath" was one of the twelve tribes of Israel, and the meaning of this phrase is most likely "upon the harp of Gath," or "according to the tune of Gath."

3. According to Mahalath עַל־מָחֲלַת ('al māhᵃlat)

Psalm 53's superscription contains this direction. Psalm 88 adds the word Leannoth לְעַנּוֹת (lᵉ 'annôt). "'al māhᵃlat (lᵉ 'annôt)" was most likely a particular melody or recitative style used with these psalms.

4. According to the Lilies עַל־שׁוֹשַׁנִּים ('al šôšannîm)

Psalm 45 and 69 indicate that this particular melody or recitative style is to be used in their performance.

5. According to the Sheminith עַל־הַשְּׁמִינִית   (*'al haššᵉ mînît*)
This direction, which is found in the superscriptions of Psalms 6 and 12, is usually left untranslated. The Hebrew word שְׁמִינִית (*šᵉ mînît*) means "eighth," so the phrase might mean "on the eight-stringed instrument" or "on the eighth octave or string."

6. According to Muthlabben /לַבֵּן עַלְמוּת (*'almût labbēn*)
The literal meaning of this mysterious phrase, which appears in the superscription of Psalm 9, is "according to death, for the son."

7. According to the Deer of the Dawn עַל־אַיֶּלֶת הַשַּׁחַר (*'al 'ayyelet haššaḥar*) "*'al 'ayyelet haššaḥar*," which occurs only in the superscription of Psalm 22, is most likely some melodic tune or recitative style that was to be used in the singing of this psalm.

8. According to Alamoth עַל־עֲלָמוֹת   (*'al ᵃlāmôt*)
This superscription of Psalm 46 means, literally, "according to the young maidens." Again, it is most likely some melodic tune or recitative style to be used in the performance of Psalm 46.

9. According to the Dove of the Far-Off Terebinths
עַל־יוֹנַת אֵלֶם רְחֹקִים (*'al yônat 'ēlem rᵉḥoqîm*)
Psalm 56's superscription is most likely a reference to a particular melodic tune or recitative style.

10. According to the Lily of the Covenant עַל־שׁוּשַׁן עֵדוּת (*'al šûšan 'ēdût*)
Again, this superscription, which is found in Psalm 60, is apparently a reference to a particular melodic tune or recitative style.

IV. Selah סֶלָה (*selāh*)

"*selāh*" occurs seventy-one times in thirty-nine psalms. It is left untranslated and appears to be a liturgical instruction, placed at key junctures in the psalms to indicate some sort of pause in the recitation. The Hebrew root of the word is most likely סָלַל (*sālal*), which means "a lifting up of the eyes or the voice." An Aramaic root *sl* means "to pray, to bow down." We may understand "*selāh*" to mean a musical interlude in which the worshiper bows in prayer or raises the hand or voice in prayer.

> While I kept silence, my body wasted away
>   through my groaning all day long.

For day and night your hand was heavy upon me;
    my strength was dried up as by the heat of summer.
                    Selah

Then I acknowledged my sin to you,
    and I did not hide my iniquity;
I said, "I will confess my transgressions to the LORD,"
    and you forgave the guilt of my sin.
                    Selah

Therefore let all who are faithful
    offer prayer to you;
at a time of distress, the rush of mighty waters
    shall not reach them.
You are a hiding place for me;
    you preserve me from trouble;
    you surround me with glad cries of deliverance.
                    Selah (32:3–7)

Michael Goulder has suggested that "*selāh*" means something like "recitative" and marks a pause in the psalm at which there should be the recitation of a prayer or a story from ancient Israel's history. At the "*selāh*" in Psalm 85:2, for example, the worshipers or priest would recite a portion of Exodus 32–34 in the following manner.

LORD, you were favorable to your land;
    you restored the fortunes of Jacob.
You forgave the iniquity of your people;
    you pardoned all their sin. (Ps. 85:1–2)

(According to Exodus 32, after the people made the golden calf and worshiped it, the anger of the Lord burned against them and God determined to destroy the people. Moses came down from the mountain to observe what was happening and persuaded the Lord not to destroy the people.)

And the LORD said to Moses, "I hereby make a covenant. Before all your people I will perform marvels, such as have not been performed in all the earth or in any nation; and all the people among whom you live shall see the work of the LORD; for it is an awesome thing that I will do with you." (Ex. 34:10)

BIBLIOGRAPHY

Allen, Leslie C. *Psalms 101-150.* Word Biblical Commentary 21, edited by John D. W. Watts. Waco, Texas: Word Books, 1983.

Anderson, Bernhard W. *Out of the Depths,* 3d ed. Louisville: Westminster John Knox Press, 2000.

Arnold, Bill T., and Bryan E. Beyer, eds. *Readings from the Ancient Near East.* Encountering Biblical Studies, edited by Eugene H. Merrill. Grand Rapids: Baker Academic, 2002.

Ballard, H. Wayne, Jr., and W. Dennis Tucker, Jr., eds. *An Introduction to Wisdom Literature and the Psalms: Festschrift Marvin E. Tate.* Macon, Georgia: Mercer University Press, 2000.

Bellinger, W. H., Jr. *The Testimony of Poets and Sages: The Psalms and Wisdom Literature.* Macon, Georgia: Smyth & Helwys, 1998.

———. *Psalms: Reading and Studying the Book of Praises.* Peabody, Massachusetts: Hendrickson Publishers, 1990.

Berquist, Jon L. *Judaism in Persia's Shadow: A Social and Historical Approach.* Minneapolis: Fortress Press, 1995.

Braude, William G. *The Midrash on Psalms.* 2 vols. New Haven, Connecticut: Yale University Press, 1959.

Brown, William P. *Seeing the Psalms: A Theology of Metaphor.* Louisville: Westminster John Knox Press, 2002.

Brueggemann, Walter. *Abiding Astonishment: Psalms, Modernity, and the Making of History.* Literary Currents in Biblical Interpretation, edited by Danna Nolan Fewell and David M. Gunn. Louisville: Westminster/John Knox Press, 1991.

———. *Finally Comes the Poet: Daring Speech for Proclamation.* Philadelphia: Fortress Press, 1989.

———. *Israel's Praise: Doxology against Idolatry and Ideology.* Philadelphia: Fortress Press, 1988.

———. *The Psalms and the Life of Faith.* Edited by Patrick D. Miller. Minneapolis: Fortress Press, 1995.

Brueggemann, Walter, and Patrick D. Miller, Jr. "Psalm 73 as a Canonical Marker." *JSOT* 72 (1996): 45–56.

Clifford, Richard J. *Psalms 1-72.* Abingdon Old Testament Commentaries, edited by Patrick D. Miller. Nashville: Abingdon Press, 2002.

Craigie, Peter C. *Psalms 1-50.* Word Biblical Commentary 19, edited by John D. W. Watts. Waco, Texas: Word Books, 1983.

Crenshaw, James L. *The Psalms: An Introduction.* Grand Rapids: Wm. B. Eerdmans, 2001.

Crow, Loren D. *The Songs of Ascents (Psalms 120-134): Their Place in Israelite History and Religion.* SBL Dissertation Series 148, edited by Michael V. Fox. Atlanta: Scholars Press, 1996.

Davidson, Robert. *The Vitality of Worship: A Commentary on the Book of Psalms.* Grand Rapids: Wm. B. Eerdmans, 1998.

deClaissé-Walford, Nancy L. *Reading from the Beginning: The Shaping of the Hebrew Psalter.* Macon, Georgia: Mercer University Press, 1997.

Flint, Peter W. *The Dead Sea Psalms Scrolls and the Book of Psalms.* Studies on the Texts of the Desert of Judah, edited by F. Garcia Martinez and A. S. Van der Woude. Leiden: Brill, 1997.

Flint, Peter W., and Patrick D. Miller, Jr., eds. *The Book of Psalms: Composition and Reception.* Vetus Testamentum Supplementum Series. Leiden: E. J. Brill, 2003.

Fokkelman, J. P. *Reading Biblical Poetry: An Introductory Guide.* Translated by Ineke Smit. Louisville: Westminster John Knox Press, 2001.

Freedman, David Noel. *Psalm 119: The Exaltation of Torah.* Biblical and Judaic Studies 6, edited by William Henry Propp. Winona Lake, Indiana: Eisenbrauns, 1999.

Gerstenberger, Erhard S. *Psalms, Part 1: With an Introduction to Cultic Poetry.* The Forms of the Old Testament Literature 14, edited by Rolf Knierim and Gene M. Tucker. Grand Rapids: Wm. B. Eerdmans, 1988.

———. *Psalms, Part 2, and Lamentations.* The Forms of the Old Testament Literature 15, edited by Rolf Knierim, Gene M. Tucker, and Marvin A. Sweeney. Grand Rapids: Wm. B. Eerdmans, 2001.

Goulder, Michael D. *The Psalms of the Return (Book V, Psalms 107-150).* JSOT Supplement Series 258, edited by David J. A. Clines and Philip R. Davies. Sheffield: Sheffield Academic Press, 1998.

———. *The Psalms of the Sons of Korah.* JSOT Supplement Series 20. Sheffield: Sheffield Academic Press, 1982.

Gunkel, Hermann. *An Introduction to the Psalms: The Genres of the Religious Lyric of Israel.* Mercer Library of Biblical Studies. Translated by James D. Nogalski. Macon, Georgia: Mercer University Press, 1998.

———. *The Psalms: A Form-Critical Introduction.* Fact Books Biblical Series, translated by Thomas M. Horner. Philadelphia: Fortress Press, 1967.

Holladay, William L. *The Psalms through Three Thousand Years: Prayerbook of a Cloud of Witnesses*. Minneapolis: Fortress Press, 1993.

Howard, David M., Jr. *The Structure of Psalms 93-100*. Biblical and Judaic Studies 5, edited by William Henry Propp. Winona Lake, Indiana: Eisenbrauns, 1997.

Jinkins, Michael. *In the House of the Lord: Inhabiting the Psalms of Lament*. Collegeville, Minnesota: The Liturgical Press, 1998.

Josephus, Flavius. *The Works of Josephus*. Translated by William Whiston. Peabody, Massachusetts: Hendrickson Publishers, 1987.

Kraus, Hans-Joachim. *Psalms 1-59: A Commentary*. Translated by Hilton C. Oswald. Minneapolis: Augsburg Publishing House, 1988.

———. *Psalms 60-150: A Commentary*. Translated by Hilton C. Oswald. Minneapolis: Fortress Press, 1993.

———. *Theology of the Psalms*. Translated by Keith Crim. Minneapolis: Fortress Press, 1992.

Lichtheim, Miriam. *Ancient Egyptian Literature*. 3 vols. Berkeley: University of California Press, 1973, 1976, 1980.

Limburg, James. *Psalms*. Westminster Bible Companion, edited by Patrick D. Miller and David L. Bartlett. Louisville: Westminster John Knox Press, 2000.

Mays, James Luther. "The David of the Psalms." *Interpretation* 40 (1986): 143–55.

———. *The Lord Reigns: A Theological Handbook to the Psalms*. Louisville: Westminster John Knox Press, 1994.

———. "The Place of the Torah-Psalms in the Psalter." *JBL* 106/1 (1987): 3–12.

———. *Psalms*. Interpretation: A Bible Commentary for Teaching and Preaching, edited by Patrick D. Miller, Jr. Louisville: Westminster John Knox Press, 1994.

McCann, J. Clinton, Jr. "The Book of Psalms," in *The New Interpreter's Bible: A Commentary in Twelve Volumes,* vol. 4, edited by Leander E. Keck, 641–1280. Nashville: Abingdon Press, 1996.

———. "The Psalms as Instruction." *Interpretation* 46 (1992): 117–28.

———, ed. *The Shape and Shaping of the Psalter*. JSOT Supplement Series 159, edited by David J. A. Clines and Philip R. Davies. Sheffield: JSOT Press, 1993.

———. *A Theological Introduction to the Book of Psalms: The Psalms as Torah*. Nashville: Abingdon Press, 1993.

McCann, J. Clinton, Jr., and James C. Howell. *Preaching the Psalms*. Nashville: Abingdon Press, 2001.

Miller, Patrick D., Jr. *Interpreting the Psalms*. Philadelphia: Fortress Press, 1986.

———. "The End of the Psalter: A Response to Erich Zenger." *JSOT* 80 (1998): 103–10.

Morgan, Donn F. *Between Text and Community: The "Writings" in Canonical Interpretation*. Minneapolis: Fortress Press, 1990.

Mowinckel, Sigmund. *The Psalms in Israel's Worship*. 2 vols. Translated by D. R. Ap-Thomas. Nashville: Abingdon Press, 1962.

Pritchard, James B., ed. *Ancient Near Eastern Texts Relating to the Old Testament*. 3d ed. Princeton: Princeton University Press, 1969.

Reid, Stephen Breck. *Listening In: A Multicultural Reading of the Psalms*. Nashville: Abingdon Press, 1997.

———, ed. *Psalms and Practice: Worship, Virtue, and Authority*. Collegeville, Minnesota: The Liturgical Press, 2001.

Sanders, James A. *The Dead Sea Psalms Scroll*. Ithaca, New York: Cornell University Press, 1967.

———. *From Sacred Story to Sacred Text*. Philadelphia: Fortress Press, 1987.

Sarna, Nahum M. *On the Book of Psalms: Exploring the Prayers of Ancient Israel*. New York: Schocken Books, 1993.

Sheppard, Gerald T. "Theology and the Book of Psalms." *Interpretation* 46 (1992): 143–55.

Smith, Mark S. "The Levitical Compilation of the Psalter." *ZAW* 103 (1991): 258–63.

———. "The Psalms as a Book for Pilgrims." *Interpretation* 46 (1992): 156–66.

Tanner, Beth LaNeel. *The Book of Psalms through the Lens of Intertextuality*. Studies in Biblical Literature 26, edited by Hemchand Gossai. New York: Peter Lang, 2001.

Tate, Marvin E. *Psalms 51-100*. Word Biblical Commentary 20, edited by John D. W. Watts. Dallas: Word Books, 1990.

Terrien, Samuel. *The Psalms: Strophic Structure and Theological Commentary*. Grand Rapids: Wm. B. Eerdmans, 2003.

Westermann, Claus. *Praise and Lament in the Psalms*. Translated by Keith R. Crim and Richard N. Soulen. Atlanta: John Knox Press, 1981.

———. *The Psalms: Structure, Content and Message*. Translated by Ralph D. Gehrke. Minneapolis: Augsburg Publishing House, 1980.

Wilson, Gerald Henry. *The Editing of the Hebrew Psalter*. SBL Dissertation Series 76, edited by J. J. M. Roberts. Chico, California: Scholars Press, 1985.

———. "Evidence of Editorial Divisions in the Hebrew Psalter." *Vetus Testamentum* 34 (1984): 337–52.

———. "The Qumran Psalms Manuscripts and the Consecutive Arrangement of Psalms in the Hebrew Psalter." *CBQ* 45 (1983): 377–88.

———. "The Shape of the Book of Psalms." *Interpretation* 46 (1992): 129–42.

———. "The Use of Royal Psalms at the 'Seams' of the Hebrew Psalter." *JSOT* 35 (1986): 85–94.

———. "The Use of 'Untitled' Psalms in the Hebrew Psalter." *ZAW* 97 (1985): 404–13.

Zenger, Erich. *A God of Vengeance? Understanding the Psalms of Divine Wrath.* Translated by Linda M. Maloney. Louisville: Westminster John Knox Press, 1996.

———. "The Composition and Theology of the Fifth Book of Psalms, Psalms 107-145." *JSOT* 80 (1998): 77–102.

ABBREVIATIONS IN NOTES

CahRB   Cahiers de la Revue biblique
CBQ   *Catholic Biblical Quarterly*
CBQMS   Catholic Biblical Quarterly Monograph Series
CRBS   *Currents in Research: Biblical Studies*
CurTM   *Currents in Theology and Mission*
FM   *Faith and Mission*
FO   *Folia orientalia*
FOTL   Forms of the Old Testament Literature
HBT   *Horizons in Biblical Theology*
JBL   *Journal of Biblical Literature*
JBT   *Jahrbuch für Biblische Theologie*
JNSL   *Journal of Northwest Semitic Languages*
JSOT   *Journal for the Study of the Old Testament*
JSOTSup   Journal for the Study of the Old Testament:
                 Supplement Series
NEchtB   Neue Echter Bibel
PRS   *Perspectives in Religious Studies*
ResQ   *Restoration Quarterly*
SBLDS   Society of Biblical Literature Dissertation Series
SJOT   *Scandinavian Journal of the Old Testament*
TLZ   *Theologische Literaturzeitung*
TZ   *Theologische Zeitschrift*
VeE   *Verbum et Ecclesia*
VTSup   Vetus Testamentum Supplements
WBC   Word Biblical Commentary
ZAW   *Zeitschrift für die alttestamentliche Wissenschaft*

NOTES

Introduction

[1]William G. Braude, *The Midrash on Psalms,* vol. 1 (New Haven, Conn.: Yale Univ. Press, 1959), 230.

[2]See the wonderful and thorough treatment of the use of psalms in William L. Holladay, *The Psalms through Three Thousand Years: Prayerbook of a Cloud of Witnesses* (Minneapolis: Fortress Press, 1993).

[3]*The Revised Common Lectionary: The Consultation on Common Texts* (Nashville: Abingdon Press, 1992).

[4]Nahum M. Sarna, *On the Book of Psalms: Exploring the Prayers of Ancient Israel* (New York: Schocken Books, 1993), 3.

[5]Dietrich Bonhoeffer, *Life Together/Prayerbook of the Bible,* Dietrich Bonhoeffer Works, vol. 5, trans. Daniel W. Bloesh and James H. Burtness, ed. Geffrey B. Kelly (Minneapolis: Fortress Press, 1996), 147.

[6]See, for example, the comments of Hans-Joachim Kraus, *Psalms 1–59: A Commentary* (Minneapolis: Augsburg, 1988), and Peter C. Craigie, *Psalms 1–50,* Word Biblical Commentary 19 (Waco, Tex.: Word Books, 1983).

[7]See Kraus, *Psalms 1–59,* 453, and Craigie, *Psalms 1–50,* 338.

[8]See Craigie, *Psalms 1–50,* 322, and Mitchell Dahood, *Psalms II: 51–100,* The Anchor Bible (New York: Doubleday, 1968), 263.

[9]See Dahood, *Psalms II: 51–100,* 199 and 250, and Marvin E. Tate, *Psalms 51–100,* Word Biblical Commentary 20 (Waco, Tex.: Word Books, 1990), 299.

[10]See the discussion in Leslie C. Allen, *Psalms 101–150,* Word Biblical Commentary 21 (Waco, Tex.: Word Books, 1983), 139–41.

[11]See Nancy L. deClaissé-Walford, *Reading from the Beginning: The Shaping of the Hebrew Psalter* (Macon, Ga.: Mercer Univ. Press, 1997), 21–29.

Chapter 1: What Word Are We Reading?

[1]Emily Dickinson, "A Book," in *Collected Poems of Emily Dickinson* (New York: Avenel Books: 1982), 34.

[2]Barbara Herrenstein Smith, *Poetic Closure: A Study of How Poems End* (Chicago: The Univ. of Chicago Press, 1968), 23.

[3]Walter Brueggemann, *Finally Comes the Poet: Daring Speech for Proclamation* (Philadelphia: Fortress Press, 1989), 1.

[4]Richard Gillard, "The Servant Song," 1977.

[5]Robert Frost, "The Road Not Taken," in *Complete Poems of Robert Frost* (New York: Holt, Rinehart, and Winston, 1967).

[6]Walt Whitman, "Passage to India," 5:101–5, in *Leaves of Grass* (New York: Mentor Books, the New American Library, 1954), 324.

[7]Brueggemann, *Finally Comes the Poet,* 6.

[8]Bishop Robert Lowth, *Isaiah: A New Translation with a Preliminary Dissertation and Notes Critical, Philological, and Explanatory* (London: T. Caldell, 1824, reprint 1848; German original, 1779), introduction; compare Lowth, *De sacra poesi Hebraeorum praelectiones academicae Oxonii habitae,* 1753.

[9]For a full discussion of parallelism in Hebrew poetry, see J. P. Fokkelman, *Reading Biblical Poetry,* trans. Ineke Smit (Louisville: Westminster John Knox Press, 2001).

[10]For a good recent treatment of acrostic psalms, see David Noel Freedman, *Psalm 119: The Exaltation of Torah,* Biblical and Judaic Studies 6 (Winona Lake, Ind.: Eisenbrauns, 1999).

Chapter 2: The Forms of the Psalms

[1]For a survey of psalm research since Gunkel, see Erich Zenger, "Psalmenforschung nach Hermann Gunkel und Sigmund Mowinckel," *Congress Volume, Oslo 1998,* ed. Andrè Lemaire and

Magne SÆBØ, VTSup 80; Leiden: Brill, 2000), 399–435; and Manfred Oeming, "And er Quelle des Gebets: Neuere Untersuchungen zu den Psalmen," *TLZ* 127 (2002): 367–84.

[2]See Pss. 12, 14, 15, 24, 29, 33, 44, 46, 48, 50, 67, 68, 75, 76, 81, 82, 100, 105, 107, 113, 114, 115, 117, 124, 125, 129, 134, 135, 136, 147, 149, 150.

[3]Hermann Gunkel, *The Psalms: a Form-Critical Introduction,* Facet Books Biblical Series, trans. Thomas M. Horner (Philadelphia: Fortress Press, 1967; German original, 1930), 13.

[4]For discussion of the structure and formal elements of each psalm, see Erhard S. Gerstenberger, *Psalms,* FOTL 14, 2 Parts (Grand Rapids: Eerdmans, 1988, 2001).

[5]See Pss. 23, 30, 34, 41, 66, 84, 87, 91, 92, 103, 111, 116, 118, 121, 122, 131, 138, 139, 146.

[6]Gunkel, *The Psalms,* vol. 1, 17; note that Gunkel called this the Individual Thank Offering Song; compare Gerstenberger, pt. 1, 14–16.

[7]W. H. Bellinger, Jr., *Psalms: Reading and Studying the Book of Praises* (Peabody, Mass.: Hendrickson Publishers, 1990), 76. Erhard Gerstenberger proposes a four-part structure for the community hymn: (1) calling on Yahweh; (2) summons to praise; (3) praise of Yahweh because of his works, deeds, and qualities; and (4) blessings and wishes. See Gerstenberger, *Psalms,* pt. 1, 17.

[8]For Gerstenberger's more detailed breakdown of the psalm, see Psalms, pt. 1, 143–46.

[9]See Kathrin Ehlers, "Wege aus der Vergessenheit. Zu einem neuen Sammelband zum Thema 'Klage,'" *JBT* 16 (2001): 383–96.

[10]See Pss. 12, 14, 44, 53, 58, 60, 74, 79, 80, 83, 85, 90, 106, 108, 123, 126, 137.

[11]See Pss. 3, 4, 5, 6, 7, 9, 10, 11, 13, 16, 17, 22, 25, 26, 27, 28, 31, 35, 36, 38, 39, 40, 42, 43, 51, 52, 54, 55, 56, 57, 59, 61, 62, 63, 64, 69, 70, 71, 77, 86, 88, 94, 102, 109, 120, 130, 140, 141, 142, 143.

[12]Gunkel, *The Psalms,* 20.

[13]Gunkel, *The Psalms,* 21, discusses three elements of the individual lament: invocation, body with laments or supplication, and concluding vows. Bellinger, in *Psalms,* 45–46, cites four elements in a lament psalm: invocation, complaint, petition, and expression of confidence. This fourfold division is a simplification of his previous six-element analysis, found in *Psalmody and Prophecy,* JSOT Supplement Series 27 (Sheffield, U.K.: JSOT Press, 1984), 22–24. James Limburg, in *Psalms,* Westminster Bible Companion (Louisville: Westminster John Knox Press, 2000), 8, cites three elements in a lament psalm: complaint, affirmation of trust, and call for help or request. J. Clinton McCann, Jr., "The Book of Psalms," in *The New Interpreter's Bible,* vol. 4 (Nashville: Abingdon Press, 1996), 644–45, outlines five elements: opening address, description of trouble or distress, plea or petition to God, profession of trust or confidence in God, and promise or vow to praise God or to offer a sacrifice. Gerstenberger, *Psalms,* pt. 1, 10–14, separates laments or dirges from complaints. Dirges have five elements: Moaning and wailing, description of catastrophe, reference to former bliss, call to weep and wail, and subdued plea. I have adopted a fivefold format for the lament, but with somewhat different category titles than McCann uses: invocation, complaint, petition, expression of trust, and expression of praise. This is modified from my own previous four-fold division. See Nancy L. deClaissé-Walford, *Reading from the Beginning: The Shaping of the Hebrew Psalter* (Macon, Ga.: Mercer Univ. Press, 1997), 50.

[14]Gerstenberger, *Psalms,* pt. 1, 12, lists the following basic elements of his complaints, in which he places Psalm 6: invocation (v. 1), complaint (vv. 5–7), confession of sin or assertion of innocence, affirmation of confidence, plea or petition for help (vv. 1*b*–4), imprecation against enemies (vv. 8–10), acknowledgment of divine response 8*b*–9), vow or pledge, hymnic elements or blessings, anticipated thanksgiving.

[15]See Pss. 2, 18, 20, 21, 45, 72, 89, 101, 110, 132, 144; for a recent study of the royal psalms, see Randy G. Haney, *Text and Concept in Royal Psalms,* Studies in Biblical Literature 30 (Frankfurt am Main: Lang, 2002).

[16]See Pss. 8, 19, 65, 104.

[17]See Pss. 1, 32, 49, 73, 78, 112, 119, 127, 128, 133, 145; for a skeptical approach to the category of wisdom psalms, see James L. Crenshaw, "Wisdom Psalms," *CR: BS* 8 (2000): 9–17.

[18]See Ps. 47, 95, 96, 97, 98, 99.

[19]See Hermann Gunkel, *Introduction to Psalms: The Genres of the Religious Lyric of Israel,* trans. James D. Nogalski (Macon, Ga.: Mercer Univ. Press, 1998; German original, 1933), particularly 319–32.

[20]James A. Sanders, "Adaptable for Life: The Nature and Function of Canon," in *From Sacred Story to Sacred Text* (Philadelphia: Fortress Press, 1987), 16.

Chapter 3: The Shape of the Psalter

[1]To learn more about and read any of these texts, see James B. Pritchard, ed., *Ancient Near Eastern Texts Relating to the Old Testament,* 3rd ed. (Princeton, N.J.: Princeton Univ. Press, 1969); Miriam Lichtheim, *Ancient Egyptian Literature,* vol. 1, 2, 3 (Berkeley, Calif.: Univ. of California Press, 1973, 1976, 1980); Bill T. Arnold and Bryan E. Beyer, eds., *Readings from the Ancient Near East,* Primary Sources for Old Testament Studies (Grand Rapids: Baker Book House, 2002); and William W. Hallo and K. Lawson Younger, Jr., eds., *Canonical Compositions from the Biblical World,* The Context of Scripture, vol. 1 (Leiden: Brill, 1997).

[2]Norman Gottwald, *The Hebrew Bible: A Socio-Literary Introduction* (Philadelphia: Fortress Press, 1985), 14.

[3]The last line is from the *New American Standard Bible.*

[4]James A. Sanders, *The Dead Sea Psalms Scroll* (Ithaca, N.Y.: Cornell Univ. Press, 1967), 87.

[5]William G. Braude, *The Midrash on Psalms* (New Haven, Conn.: Yale Univ. Press, 1959), 1:6.

[6]See Harry F. van Rooy, "The Headings of the Psalms in the Dead Sea Scrolls," *JNSL* 28 (2002): 127–41.

[7]See chapter 2 for a full discussion of these terms.

[8]While Pss. 10 and 33 do not have superscriptions, both have been shown to have strong links to the psalms preceding them (9 and 32), and may have at one time been single units rather than separate psalms.

[9]See James Nogalski's discussion of the Elohistic Psalter in his essay "From Psalm to Psalms to Psalter," in *An Introduction to Wisdom Literature and the Psalms: A Festschrift in Honor of Marvin Tate,* ed. H. Wayne Ballard and W. Dennis Tucker (Macon, Ga.: Mercer Univ. Press, 2000), 44–46.

[10]For a recent survey and study of the collection and shaping of the Psalter see Jean-Marie Auwers, *La Composition Littéraire du Psautier: Un Etat de la Question,* CahRB 4 (Paris: Gabalda, 2000).

[11]Ps. 18: 2, 3, 6, 27, 35, 41 (twice), 46, 50; Ps. 20: 5, 6 (twice), 9; Ps. 21: 1, 5; Ps. 22:1, 21.

[12]*Nāṣal* occurs in Ps. 18:superscription, 17, 48; Ps. 22:8, 20. *Pālaṭ* occurs in Ps. 18:3, 43, 48; Ps. 22:5, 8.

[13]See William G. Braude, *The Midrash on Psalms,* vol. 1 (New Haven, Conn.: Yale Univ. Press, 1959), 322.

[14]See chapter 2.

[15]Nahum Sarna, *On the Book of Psalms* (New York: Schocken Books, 1993), 103.

[16]*Mishnah Tractate Tamid,* 7:4. The psalms read were: Sunday—Ps. 24; Monday—Ps. 48; Tuesday—Ps. 82; Wednesday—Ps. 94; Thursday—Ps. 81; Friday—Ps. 93; Saturday—Ps. 92. The superscription to Ps. 24 (23) in the Septuagint reads, "a psalm of David, the one for the Sabbath."

[17]For a full treatment of the connections between Pss. 22, 23, and 24, see Nancy L. deClaissé-Walford, "An Intertextual Reading of Psalms 22, 23, and 24," in *The Book of Psalms: Composition and Reception,* Supplements to *Vetus Testamentum,* ed. Peter W. Flint and Patrick D. Miller (Leiden: Brill, 2002), 2004.

[18]For more information on the Dead Sea Psalm Scrolls, see James A. Sanders, *The Dead Sea Psalms Scroll;* and Peter W. Flint, *The Dead Sea Psalms Scrolls and the Bible,* Studies on the Texts of the Desert of Judah, v. 17 (Leiden: E. J. Brill, 1997).

[19]William G. Braude, *The Midrash on Psalms,* vol. 1 (New Haven, Conn.: Yale Univ. Press, 1959), 5.

Chapter 4: The History behind the Shaping of the Psalter

[1]William G. Braude, *The Midrash on Psalms,* vol. 1 (New Haven, Conn.: Yale Univ. Press, 1959), 3:2.

[2]See Nancy L. deClaissé-Walford, *Reading from the Beginning: The Shaping of the Hebrew Psalter* (Macon, Ga.: Mercer Univ. Press, 1997), 15–35; Gerald H. Wilson, *The Editing of the Hebrew Psalter,* SBLDS 76 (Chico, Calif.: Scholars Press, 1985); and Gerald H. Wilson, "A First Century C.E. Date for the Closing of the Book of Psalms?" *JBQ* 28 (2000): 102–10.

[3]For the full text of this document, see James B. Pritchard, Jr., *Ancient Near Eastern Texts Relating to the Old Testament,* 3d ed. (Princeton, N.J.: Princeton Univ. Press, 1969), 316, or Bill T. Arnold and Bryan E. Beyer, *Readings from the Ancient Near East* (Grand Rapids: Baker Academic,

2002), 147–49, or Mordechai Cogan, "Cyrus Cylinder," in *Monumental Inscriptions from the Biblical World,* The Context of Scripture, vol. 2, ed. William W. Hallo and K. Lawson Younger, Jr. (Leiden: Brill, 2000), 314–16.

[4]See also Ezra 6:3–5.

[5]For references to Zerubbabel, see 1 Chr. 3:16–19; Ezra 2:2; 3:2, 8; 4:2, 3; 5:2; Hag. 1:1; 2:21–23; and Zech. 4:6–10.

[6]The last mention of Zerubbabel is in Zech. 4, which may date to February 519. See Frederick J. Murphy, *Early Judaism: The Exile to the Time of Jesus* (Peabody, Mass.: Hendrickson Publishers, 2002) and David L. Petersen, "Zerubbabel and Jerusalem Temple Reconstruction," *CBQ* 36 (1974): 366–72.

[7]Flavius Josephus, *The Antiquities of the Jews,* in *The Works of Josephus,* trans. William Whiston (Peabody, Mass.: Hendrickson, 1987), XI.307, 337–38. Peter Schäfer, in "The Hellenistic and Maccabaean Periods," in *Israelite and Judaean History* (London: SCM Press, 1977), 596, points out that it is unlikely that Alexander actually paid a visit to Jerusalem. The high priest of Jerusalem readily submitted, on behalf of all the people, to his rule, so he "left untouched the organizational structure of Judah."

[8]Josephus, *Antiquities,* XII.138–41, 317.

[9]Much of the motivation for Antiochus IV's actions may have been economic. The Seleucid Empire needed funds to pay tribute to a growing power in the West, Rome. The book of 2 Maccabees describes an incident in which the Seleucid king ordered that money in the treasury of the temple at Jerusalem be confiscated as part of the religious controls placed upon Judaism. See 2 Macc. 3:4–13.

[10]Josephus, *Antiquities,* XII. 417–19, 334. See also 1 Macc. 8:17–30.

[11]Jacob Neusner, *Self-Fulfilling Prophecy: Exile and Return in the History of Judaism* (Atlanta: Scholars Press, 1990), 9.

[12]James A. Sanders, "Adaptable for Life: The Nature and Function of Canon," in *From Sacred Story to Sacred Text* (Philadelphia: Fortress Press, 1987), 18.

[13]Walter Brueggemann, *Israel's Praise: Doxology against Idolatry and Ideology* (Philadelphia: Fortress Press, 1988), 13.

[14]Sanders, "Adaptable for Life," 18.

Chapter 5: Book One of the Psalter

[1]See appendix 2 for the meanings of the technical terms in the superscriptions.

[2]The *New Revised Standard Version Bible* has changed the singular pronoun in Ps. 1 to plural to better render the psalm in inclusive language. I have maintained the Hebrew singular to emphasize the individuality of the message of this psalm.

[3]James L. Mays, *Psalms,* Interpretation: A Bible Commentary for Teaching and Preaching (Louisville: John Knox Press, 1994), 15; for bibliography on each individual psalm, see Erhard S. Gerstenberger, *Psalms,* FOTL, vols. 14, 15 (Grand Rapids: Eerdmans, 1988, 2001).

[4]Patrick Miller, "The Beginning of the Psalter," in *The Shape and Shaping of the Psalter,* ed. J. Clinton McCann, Jr., JSOT Sup 159 (Sheffield, UK: JSOT Press, 1993), 88, claims that a major function of Ps. 2 read after Ps. 1 is the setting of the category of the wicked "under the rubric 'enemies.'"

[5]See the essays in Eckart Otto and Erich Zenger, eds., *"Mein Sohn bist du" (Ps 2,7). Studien zu den Konigspsalmen* (SBS 192: KBW, 2002); J. J. M. Roberts, "The Enthronement of Yhwh and David: The Abiding Theological Significance of the Kingship Language of the Psalms," *CBQ* 64 (2002): 657–86.

[6]Frank-Lothar Hossfeld and Erich Zenger, *Die Psalmen I, Psalm 1–50,* NEchtB (Wurzburg: Echter Verlag, 1993), 49, maintain that the order of the sections of Ps. 2 correspond to the ritual of an enthronement ceremony. See also James L. Mays, *The Lord Reigns: A Theological Handbook to the Psalms* (Louisville: Westminster/John Knox Press, 1994), 111–13.

[7]See 2 Kgs. 11:12. For a description of an enthronement ceremony, see Sigmund Mowinckel, *The Psalms in Israel's Worship,* vol. 1, trans. D. R. Ap-Thomas (New York: Abingdon Press, 1962), 61–76; and J. Clinton McCann, Jr., "The Book of Psalms," in *The New Interpreter's Bible,* vol. 4, ed. Leander E. Keck (Nashville: Abingdon Press, 1996), 689.

[8]For full treatments of the issue, see, among others, Hans-Joachim Kraus, *Psalms 1–59: A Commentary,* trans. H. C. Oswald (Minneapolis: Augsburg, 1988), 124–35; and McCann, "The Book of Psalms," 688–90.

[9]Although Ps. 10 does not have a superscription in the Masoretic Text, it is strongly linked to Ps. 9, a "psalm of David." In the Septuagint, Pss. 9 and 10 are joined together as a single psalm, McCann, "The Book of Psalms," 713–20. By the same token, Ps. 33, which has no superscription in the Masoretic Text but is titled "a psalm of David" in the Septuagint, has strong linguistic links with Ps. 32. See McCann, 808–12.

[10]See Gerald H. Wilson, "The Use of Untitled Psalms in the Hebrew Psalter," *ZAW* 97 (1985): 404–13.

[11]McCann, "The Book of Psalms," 689. See also Harold E. Hosch, "Psalms 1 and 2: A Discourse Analysis," *Notes on Translation* 15 (2001), 4–12; J. Clinton McCann, Jr., "Righteousness, Justice, and Peace: A Contemporary Theology of the Psalms," *HBT* 23 (2001): 111–31; Jesper Hogenhaven, "The Opening of the Psalter: A Study in Jewish Theology," *SJOT* 15 (2001): 169–80; and Robert Cole, "An Integrated Reading of Psalms 1 and 2," *JSOT* 98 (2002): 75–88.

[12]See James D. Nogalski, "Reading David in the Psalter: A Study in Liturgical Hermeneutics," *HBT* 23 (2001): 168–91.

[13]James L. Mays, "The David of the Psalms," *Interpretation* 40 (1986): 145.

[14]Peter C. Craigie, *Psalms 1–50,* Word Biblical Commentary 19 (Waco, Tex.: Word Books, 1983), 107; compare Marvin E. Tate, "An Exposition of Psalm 8," *PRS* 28 (2001): 343–59.

[15]James L. Mays, "The Place of the Torah-Psalms in the Psalter," *JBL* 106/1 (1987): 3.

Chapter 6: Book Two of the Psalter

[1]See appendix 2 for the meanings of the technical terms in the superscriptions.

[2]Note the unusual approach of Laura Joffe, "The Answer to the Meaning of Life, the Universe, and the Elohistic Psalter," *JSOT* 27 (2002): 223–35.

[3]For a full discussion of the Korahites, see Michael Goulder, *The Psalms of the Sons of Korah,* JSOT Sup 20 (Sheffield, UK: JSOT Press, 1982).

[4]For the full text of the story, see Miriam Lichtheim, *Ancient Egyptian Literature,* vol. 1 (Berkeley, Calif.: Univ. of California Press, 1973), 163–69; and James B. Pritchard, ed., *Ancient Near Eastern Texts Relating to the Old Testament,* 3d ed. (Princeton, N.J.: Princeton Univ. Press, 1969), 405–7.

[5]For an excellent treatment of water imagery in the book of Psalms, see William P. Brown, *Seeing the Psalms* (Louisville: Westminster John Knox Press, 2002), 105–34.

[6]See, for example, Hans-Joachin Kraus, *Psalms 1–59: A Commentary,* trans. H. C. Oswald (Minneapolis: Augsburg Publishing House, 1988), 435–42; Gerald H. Wilson, *The Editing of the Hebrew Psalter,* SBLDS 76 (Chico, Calif.: Scholars Press, 1985), 176–77; and J. Clinton McCann, Jr., "The Book of Psalms," in *The New Interpreter's Bible,* vol. 4, ed. Leander E. Keck (Nashville: Abingdon Press, 1996), 852–54.

[7]Ps. 44 is the first community lament in the Psalter.

[8]Erhard Gerstenberger, in *Psalms, Part 1, with an Introduction to Cultic Poetry,* FOTL 14 (Grand Rapids: Eerdmans, 1988), 210, maintains that Ps. 50 is a postexilic composition that was used in synagogue worship.

[9]Brevard Childs, *Introduction to the Old Testament as Scripture* (Philadelphia: Fortress Press, 1979), 520–22.

[10]See James D. Nogalski, "Reading David in the Psalter: A Study in Liturgical Hermeneutics," *HBT* 23 (2001): 168–91.

[11]James A. Sanders, "Canonical Context and Canonical Criticism," in *From Sacred Story to Sacred Text* (Philadelphia: Fortress Press, 1987), 170.

[12]Patrick D. Miller, Jr., *Interpreting the Psalms* (Philadelphia: Fortress Press, 1986), 53.

[13]See, for instance, the subtitles in *The New American Standard Bible: Updated Version* (Anaheim, Calif.: Foundation Publications, Inc., 1995) and in *The Good News Bible* (New York: American Bible Society, 1992). H.-J. Kraus, in *Psalms 60–150: A Continental Commentary,* trans. Hilton C. Oswald (Minneapolis: Fortress Press, 1993), 69, titles the psalm "Cast Me Not Away in the Time of Old Age."

[14]The other is Ps. 127, one of Book Five's "Songs of Ascents." See D. J. Human, "An ideal for leadership—Psalm 72: The (wise) king—Royal mediation of God's universal reign," *VeE* 23 (2003): 658–77.

[15]Kraus, *Psalms 60–150*, 76–77. McCann, in *The Book of Psalms*, 963, writes: "It is possible that the psalm was actually written for Solomon. We simply cannot date the psalm with any certainly, but it is likely that it was written for use at the coronation of Davidic kings in Jerusalem, in which case it would have been used repeatedly, along with the other royal psalms."

[16]Childs, *Introduction to the Old Testament as Scripture*, 516.

[17]Gerald H. Wilson, *Psalms Vol. 1*, the NIV Application Commentary (Grand Rapids: Zondervan, 2002), 985.

Chapter 7: Book Three of the Psalter

[1]See appendix 2 for the meanings of the technical terms in the superscriptions.

[2]See John P. Nordin, "'There is Nothing on Earth That I Desire': A Commentary on Psalm 73," *CurTM* 29 (2002): 258–64; and Corin Mihaila, "The Theological and Canonical Place of Psalm 73," *FM* 18 (2001): 52–59.

[3]Two excellent treatments of wisdom and the biblical wisdom literature are John G. Gammie and Leo G. Perdue, eds., *The Sage in Israel and the Ancient Near East* (Winona Lake, Ind.: Eisenbrauns, 1990), and Roland E. Murphy, *The Tree of Life: An Exploration of Biblical Wisdom Literature* (Grand Rapids: Eerdmanns, 1996).

[4]Miriam Lichtheim, *Ancient Egyptian Literature*, vol. 1 (Berkeley: Univ. of California Press, 1973), 177; compare Nili Shupak, "The Eloquent Peasant," *Canonical Compositions from the Biblical World*, The Context of Scripture, vol. 1, ed. William W. Hallo and K. Lawson Younger, Jr. (Brill: Leiden, 1997), 98–104.

[5]James B. Pritchard, ed., *Ancient Near Eastern Texts Relating to the Old Testament*, 3d ed. (Princeton, N.J.: Princeton Univ. Press, 1969), 435–40 and 601–4; compare Benjamin R. Foster, "The Babylonian Theodicy," in *Canonical Compositions from the Biblical World*, The Context of Scripture, vol. 1, ed. William W. Hallo and K. Lawson Younger, Jr. (Brill: Leiden, 1997), 492–95.

[6]Walter Brueggemann, "Bounded by Praise and Obedience: The Psalms as Canon," in *The Psalms and the Life of Faith*, ed. Patrick D. Miller (Minneapolis: Fortress Press, 1995), 209.

[7]On Psalm 75 see Joseph E. Jensen, "Psalm 75: Its Poetic Context and Structure," *CBQ* 63 (2001): 416–29.

[8]Samuel Terrien, *The Psalms: Strophic Structure and Theological Commentary* (Grand Rapids: Eerdmanns, 2003), 564; compare Philip McMillion, "Psalm 78: Teaching the Next Generation," *ResQ* 43 (2001): 219–28; and Beat Weber, "Psalm78: Geschichte mit Geschiche deuten," *TZ* 56 (2000): 193–214.

[9]J. Clinton McCann, Jr., "The Book of Psalms," in *The New Interpreter's Bible*, vol. 4 (Nashville: Abingdon Press, 1996), 1019.

[10]A. F. Kirkpatrick, *The Book of Psalms*, The Cambridge Bible for Schools and Colleges (Cambridge: Univ. Press, 1902), 514–15.

[11]Arthur Weiser, *The Psalms: A Commentary*, Old Testament Library (Philadelphia: Westminster Press, 1962), 576; Marvin Tate, *Psalm 50–100*, WBC 20 (Dallas: Word Books, 1990), 379, speaks of "the artistic use of traditonal prayer language."

[12]Compare 1 Chr. 16:7–36, which combines Pss. 105:1–15; 96:1–13; 106:1, 47–48.

[13]See the structural comments of Pierre Auffret, "Ta justice dans la terre de l'oubli? Etude structurelle du Psaume 88," *FO* 37 (2001): 5–18; compare Irene Nowell, "Psalm 88: A Lesson in Lament," in *Imagery and Imagination in Biblical Literature: Essays in Honor of Aloysius Fitzgerald, F. S.C.*, ed. Lawrene Boadt and Mark S. Smith, *CBQMS* 32 (Washington, D.C.: Catholic Biblical Association of America, 2001), 105–18.

[14]For the meaning of technical terms in the Psalms superscriptions, see appendix 2.

[15]Gerald H. Wilson, "The Use of Royal Psalms at the 'Seams' of the Hebrew Psalter," *JSOT* 35 (1986): 87–88.

[16]In 538, the Persian Empire conquered the Babylonians, and Israel became its vassal. In the late fourth century B.C.E., Alexander the Great conquered Palestine, and the Israelites became subject to Hellenistic rule. And in 63 B.C.E., the Romans conquered Jerusalem.

Chapter 8: Book Four of the Psalter

[1]We might say that the major characters in Books One, Two, and Three were the people of Israel and the Davidic king.

[2]See appendix 2 for the meanings of the technical terms in the superscriptions.

[3]Interestingly, the two words used in this verse to refer to humans—"human beings"—אֱנוֹשׁ (ʾĕnôš)—and "mortals"—בֶּן אָדָם (ben ʾādām)—are the same two words that are used in Psalm 8:4:

What are human beings—אֱנוֹשׁ (ʾĕnôš)—that you are mindful of them,

mortals—בֶּן אָדָם (ben ʾādām)—that you care for them?

[4]In the Book of Numbers, the Israelites again complain, and this time they say, "We remember the fish we used to eat in Egypt for nothing, the cucumbers, the melons, the leeks, the onions, and the garlic; but now our strength is dried up, and there is nothing at all but this manna to look at!" (Num. 11:5–7)

[5]Remember that we distinguish enthronement psalms from royal psalms by their subject matters—God versus the human king.

[6]For a full description of the New Year Festival and the Feast of Tabernacles, see Sigmund Mowinckel, *The Psalms in Israel's Worship,* vol. 1, trans. D. R. Ap-Thomas (Nashville: Abingdon Press, 1962), 106–92; and Hans-Joachim Kraus, *Psalms 60–150: A Continental Commentary,* trans. Hilton C. Oswald (Minneapolis: Fortress Press, 1993), 232–33.

[7]Mowinckel, *Psalms in Israel's Worship,* 106.

[8]For an extensive treatment of the Babylonian New Year Festival, see the numerous references to "Marduk," "the *Creation Epic,*" and "the New Year Festival" in Jack M. Sasson, ed., *Civilizations of the Ancient Near East* (Peabody, Mass.: Hendrickson, 1995).

[9]For a full text of *Enuma Elish,* see Bill T. Arnold and Bryan E. Beyer, eds., *Readings from the Ancient Near East,* Primary Sources for Old Testament Study (Grand Rapids: Baker Academic, 2002), 31–50; James B. Pritchard, ed., *Ancient Near Eastern Texts Relating to the Old Testament,* 3rd ed. (Princeton, N.J.: Princeton University Press, 1969), 60–72, 501–3; and Benjamin R. Foster, "Epic of Creation (*Enuma Elish*)," in *Canonical Compositions from the Biblical World,* The Context of Scripture, ed. William W. Hallo and K. Lawson Younger, Jr., vol. 1 (Leiden: Brill, 1997), 390–402.

[10]Walter Brueggemann, *Abiding Astonishment: Psalms, Modernity, and the Making of History,* Literary Currents in Biblical Interpretation (Louisville: Westminster/John Knox Press, 1991), 16–17.

Chapter 9: Book Five of the Psalter

[1]And later the Greek Empire and still later the Roman Empire.

[2]See appendix 2 for the meanings of the technical terms in the superscriptions.

[3]Erich Zenger, "The Composition and Theology of the Fifth Book of Psalms, Psalms 107–145," *JSOT* 80 (1998): 90.

[4]Michael Goulder, *The Psalms of the Return (Book V, Psalms 107–150),* JSOT Supplement Series 258 (Sheffield: Sheffield Academic Press, 1998), 24.

[5]J. Clinton McCann, Jr., *A Theological Introduction to the Book of Psalms* (Nashville: Abingdon Press, 1993), 119.

[6]James L. Mays, *Psalms,* Interpretation: A Bible Commentary for Teaching and Preaching (Louisville: John Knox Press, 1994), 436.

[7]The Hebrew words here are the words we usually translate as human beings—בְּנֵי אָדָם (bᵉnê ʾādām).

[8]The Masoretic Text has מַלְכוּתֹן ("his kingdom"). The Septuagint and Syriac versions of the Hebrew Bible have מַלְכוּתְךָ ("your kingdom").

[9]See Walter Brueggemann, "Praise and the Psalms: A Politics of Glad Abandonment," in *The Psalms and the Life of Faith,* ed. Patrick D. Miller, Jr. (Minneapolis: Fortress Press, 1995), 112–32.

Chapter 10: How Then Shall We Read the Psalter?

[1]Henri Frankfort et al., *The Intellectual Adventure of Ancient Man: An Essay on Speculative Thought in the Ancient Near East* (Chicago: Univ. of Chicago Press, 1977), 3.

[2]Ibid.

AUTHOR INDEX

SUBJECT INDEX

A

acrostic 14, 16–17, 119, 126, 127, 141–42, 161
Alexander the Great 50–52, 164, 166
Antiochus 51–52, 164
Asah/Asaphite 33, 35–36, 41, 73, 77, 85, 86, 90–91, 93, 135, 147–48
Ascents, Songs of 35–36, 114, 120–122, 142, 149–150, 157, 166
Assyria 55, 84–85, 137

B

Babylon/Babylonians/Babylonian Empire 5, 28–29, 47–48, 56, 84–85, 89, 98–99, 105, 107, 111, 113, 123, 127–28, 137, 140, 166, 167
Babylonian exile 54, 56, 123

C

Cambyses 49
canon, canonical, canonization 5, 27, 43, 45, 55, 129, 156, 159, 162–167
chiastic structure 13–14
covenant 20–21, 28, 46, 51, 54, 63, 74, 77, 85, 90, 96–98, 101–2, 105, 109–10, 117, 121–22, 135, 137,139–40, 147–48, 154–55
creation 3, 14, 17, 25, 37, 40, 42, 59, 60, 67, 69, 70–71, 74, 80, 87, 91, 100, 115, 123, 126–28, 142, 145, 147, 149–50, 167

creator 2, 17, 72, 96, 129
Cyrus 48–49, 113, 140, 164

D

Darius 49–50
David, monarchy 1, 4, 32–33, 47, 49–50, 53–55, 63, 66–67, 69, 72–73, 75, 77, 79–80, 85–86, 91, 93–94, 96–97, 100–101
David, psalms 1, 34–36, 37–38, 41–43, 46, 59–61, 64–67, 69, 74–75, 78–83, 86, 92–94, 96–97, 101–2, 104–5, 110–111, 113–17, 124–42, 145–50, 158, 164–71
Dead Sea Scrolls 33, 41
Deuteronomistic history 32, 54, 91, 101, 135
doxology 40, 72, 83, 98, 111, 127–28, 156, 164

E

Egyptian Hallel psalms 118–19, 122, 141
Elohistic collection/Psalter 35–36, 75, 163, 165
Enthronement psalms/festivals 26, 35–36, 63, 73, 77, 83, 99, 100, 105, 108, 138, 147–49, 164, 167
Enuma Elish 31, 75, 105–7, 163, 165
exodus 4, 53, 91, 98–99, 118, 139
Ezrahite 86, 95–96, 136, 148

F

feasts 40, 105, 119–21, 141–42

SCRIPTURE INDEX

HEBREW WORDS INDEX

מִזְמוֹר לְדָוִד	mizmōr lᵉdāwid	34
מִכְתָּם	miktām	151
מֶלֶךְ	melek	126
מַלְכוּת	malkût	126
מַלְכוּתוֹ	malkûtô	126, 167
מַלְכוּתֶךָ	malkûtᵉkā	126, 167
מִצְוָה	miṣwāh	119
מַשְׂכִּיל	maśkîl	151
מָשָׁל	māšal	126
מִשְׁפָּט	mišpāṭ	119
נָחַם	nāḥam	104
נָצַל	nāṣal	37–38
נֶפֶשׁ	nepeš	75–77
סֶלָה	selāh	154
עֵדָה	ʿēdāh	119
פָּלַט	pālaṭ	37
פִּקּוּד	piqqûd	119
צַדִּיקִים	ṣᵉdîqîm	62, 87
רִיק	rîq	89
רְשָׁעִים	rᵉšāʿîm	62, 87
שׁוּב	šûb	104
שִׁיר	šîr	151
שָׂכַל	śākal	72, 151
תְּהִלָּה	tᵉhillāh	152
תּוֹרָה	tôrāh	61, 119
תְּפִלָּה	tᵉpillāh	93, 152

CPSIA information can be obtained
at www.ICGtesting.com
Printed in the USA
JSHW030830040822
28870JS00001B/11